Art Nouveau

Martin Battersby

Art Nouveau

The Colour Library of Art
Paul Hamlyn

The works in this volume are reproduced by kind permission of the following collections, galleries and museums to which they belong: Bethnal Green Museum, London (Plates 8, 9, 11, 12, 30); Emmerton-Lambert, London (Plate 3); Grosvenor Gallery, London (Plate 48); Manoukian Collection (Plate 31); Metropolitan Museum of Art, New York. Harris Brisbane Dick Fund, 1966 (Plate 1); Musée des Arts Décoratifs, Paris (Plates 6, 10, 13, 37, 42); Musée National d'Art Moderne, Paris (Plates 2, 5); Private Collections (Plates 4, 7, 14, 15, 16, 17, 18, 19, 20, 21, 22, 23, 24, 27, 29, 32, 33, 34, 35, 36, 38, 41, 43, 45, 46); Victoria and Albert Museum, London (Plates 25, 26, 28, 39, 40, 44). The following photographs were supplied by Bibliothèque Nationale, Paris (Figures 1, 2, 5); Deste Photography, London (Plates 3, 4, 7, 8, 9, 11, 12, 14, 15, 16, 17, 18, 19, 20, 21, 22, 23, 24, 25, 26, 27, 28, 30, 31, 32, 33, 34, 35, 36, 38, 39, 40, 41, 43, 44, 45, 46, 47, 48, 49, 50, 51, 52, 53, 54); Giraudon, Paris (Plate 2); Geoffrey Harper (Figure 6); Mauro Pucciarelli, Rome (Plate 29); Radio Times Hulton Picture Library, London (Figure 3); Régie Autonome des Transports Parisiens (Figure 4). Plate 5 is © by S.P.A.D.E.M. and Figure 7 © by A.D.A.G.P., Paris 1968.

Frontispiece: Lift-shaft and staircase from Le Printemps, 1880, and main entrance to the Paris Exhibition, 1900.

Published by The Hamlyn Publishing Group Limited
Hamlyn House · The Centre · Feltham · Middlesex
© by The Hamlyn Publishing Group Ltd 1969
Printed in Italy by Officine Grafiche Arnoldo Mondadori, Verona

Introduction
Notes to Illustrations

BLACK AND WHITE ILLUSTRATIONS

1-3 Le Printemps interior details and Paris Exhibition
    entrance
4 Designs for Métro entrance
5 Entrance doorway
6 Bookbinding
7 Bonnard poster

THE COLOUR PLATES

 1 Dining room
 2 Portrait of Georges Rodenbach
 3 Portrait of Sarah Bernhardt
 4 Portrait of Loie Fuller
 5 Portrait of Robert de Montesquiou
 6 Majorelle metal balustrade
 7 Vitrine with ornaments
 8 Gallé worktable
 9 Gallé firescreen
10 Charpentier cabinet
11 Majorelle inlaid tray
12 Majorelle tallboy
13 Guimard tall clock
14 Table, chair and books
15 Dressing table with ornaments
16 Portrait, bronze bust and lamps
17 Candlesticks and bronze figure
18 Wall plaque and bronze dishes
19 Bronze ornaments

20 Larche gilt bronze inkwell
21 Moreau-Vauthier wall clock
22 Three bronze dancers
23 Ice fairy
24 Silver group
25 Charpentier door furniture
26 Charpentier plaques
27 Lachenal vase
28 Three vases
29 Clément-Massier plaque
30 Five pieces of pottery
31 Rodin vase
32 Porcelain vase with ormulu base
33 Gallé and Daum vases
34 Gallé and Daum vases
35 Daum inkwell
36 Pâte-de-verre vases
37 Brooch pendant
38 Buttons and silver pill box
39 Lalique silver gilt buckle
40 Hair ornament and buckle
41 Lorgnette, cigarette case and medallions
42 Lorgnette
43 Miscellaneous jewellery
44 Silver spoons and paperknives
45 Portfolios, knife, cup and book
46 Mucha poster, lamp and bowl
47 Orazi poster
48 Decorative panel
49 De Feure print
50 De Feure print
51 De Feure print
52 De Feure print
53 Bouisset print
54 Bouisset print

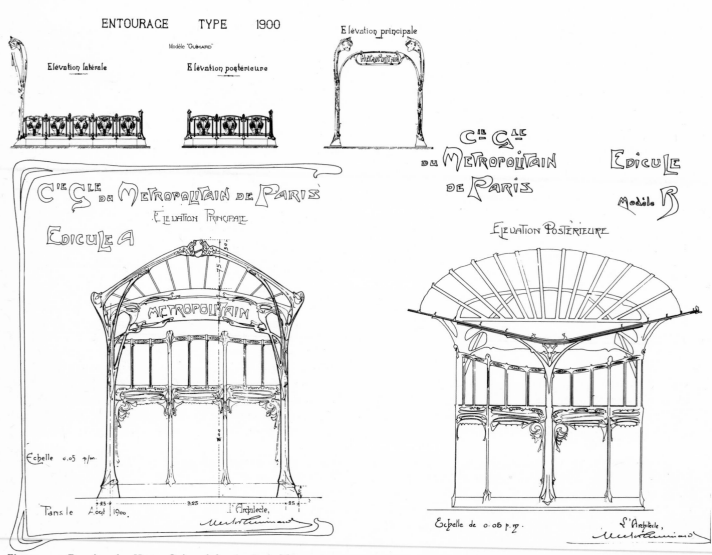

Figure 4 : Drawings by Hector Guimard for the Paris Métro entrances, 1900.

Introduction

The eminent critic and writer, Gustave Geffroy, attributed the decline in the standards of the decorative arts of France in the nineteenth century firstly to the French Revolution which broke not only the continuity of social life in France but also that of artistic life, and secondly to the carnage of the Napoleonic Wars when nearly two million Frenchmen in the prime of their lives were slaughtered. Although Napoleon is said to have remarked that the 80,000 killed at the Battle of Eylau would be replaced in Paris in one night, Geffroy considered that this sapping of the population, followed as it was by the political unrest and the lack of a stable régime during the following years, was a major factor in causing a decline in what he called 'the creative force' of the nation. France like her neighbour England had undergone the strains of an Industrial Revolution. The refinements of the Louis XVI style had coarsened during the Empire when the dictatorship of Napoleon's official artists, Percier and Fontaine, had produced a style which was an expression of the Emperor's parvenu society – pompous, derivative and ostentatious – a style reflecting the image of a brilliant ruthless adventurer. After the downfall of the Emperor the reaction against this official style with its borrowings from Rome, Greece and Egypt was a return to the Gothic – and a step backward into another past epoch rather than a step forward into the future.

The rise of a prosperous middle class created a demand for consumer goods which could be easily satisfied by machine-made products and mass production came into being. There was no place for the craftsman-designer – instead he was replaced by a machine which could produce a hundred objects in the time formerly taken to make one. Decorative motifs which had formerly been carved or chiselled by hand could be reproduced by the yard. Consequently ornament was applied with no regard for its suitability and quality of decoration was of secondary importance as long as there

was plenty of it. Every period of history was pillaged to furnish decorative motifs which were then applied haphazardly. A serious decline in creative originality and in the standards of craftsmanship was the inevitable result.

The first warning voice to be raised was that of Léon Laborde, then a Keeper at the Louvre and leader of the commission appointed by Louis Napoléon, the President of France, to supervise the French contribution to the Great Exhibition of 1851 in London. His report to the French Government condemned the low standard of design and craftsmanship which marred the French exhibits and deplored the gap which existed between artists and industry, between the fine arts and the decorative arts. This separation into two branches, he pointed out, was a new phenomenon and the blame was due to the increasing use of machinery. The remedy, he suggested, was a reorganisation of teaching in the art schools and the creation of institutions where industrial art should be taught. His ideas met with a cold reception in official circles for, as was pointed out, a considerable number of the exhibits, including those he had most strongly condemned, had received gold and silver medals and this being the case there was no need to improve any standards. Laborde's report was ignored by the authorities who were otherwise concerned with political matters but after the seizure of power by Louis Napoleon and his accession as Napoleon III, there were signs that his efforts had not been wasted and his revolutionary ideas were carried a step further when Eugène Viollet-le-Duc was appointed as one of the professors of the newly reorganised Ecole des Beaux-Arts. Viollet-le-Duc is best remembered for his restorations of medieval buildings which were severely criticised at the time; he was accused of having turned the Sainte-Chapelle into a birdcage suitable for a parrot but in this field he was probably no better and no worse than his contemporaries. His interest for us lies in his theories about architecture and decoration which were ahead of their time in that, unlike his contemporary William Morris, he did not believe that the Gothic period was the supreme manifestation of creativity and consequently unsurpassable. But he was in agreement with Morris in advocating unity in the arts and in particular in the decoration of the interior of a house. Recognising that the machine was to play a part of growing importance in everyday life he deplored the tendency to disguise the machine and its products with ornaments of an earlier age instead of devising a new idiom of design suitable for the functions of the machine itself. He foresaw the future of metal in architecture – cast iron used honestly and practically, not ornamented with Gothic fretwork or disguised as sham wood or stone.

Viollet-le-Duc was in a more favoured position than Laborde to advance his ideas with the minimum of opposition owing to the powerful protection of Princess Mathilde Napoleon whose salon he frequented. Unfortunately the abdication of the Emperor after the debâcle of the Franco-Prussian War in 1870 necessarily curtailed his influence. But the seeds had been sown. In the meantime however an event occurred on the other side of the world which was to have a profound and possibly decisive effect on French Decorative Art and one which although nobody could have realised it at the time was to bring about the flowering of Art Nouveau.

In 1893 a contributor to the magazine *Furniture and Decoration* reviewing a recent exhibition of French decorative art in London commented: 'It may be said that the industrial arts of Great Britain are at the present time under the spell of medievalism. But another and brighter mode has for several years constantly infatuated the fancy of the dainty Gaul and the influence of this inspiration pervades almost every exhibit at the Grafton Gallery. The eccentric and abiding loveliness of Japanese Art has entered into the spirit of French Decorative Art'.

In March 1854 Japan not too willingly signed a treaty with the American Commodore Perry and officially ended the seclusion which had existed since 1637 when foreigners were banished and no Japanese citizen allowed to leave the country. Contrary to belief this seclusion was not total. For twenty-eight years prior to the edict of 1637 the Dutch had had a trading post on the mainland of Japan and their honesty, fairdealing and lack of any desire to convert the Japanese to Christianity had been in sharp contrast to the Portuguese and the Spanish. The antagonism between the two Catholic communities and their conversion of large numbers of the natives had led to so much strife that the Japanese found themselves with no alternative but to banish, first the trouble-making priests, and finally the traders. The Dutch were excepted from the ban and were allowed to maintain a base, under strict supervision, on the island of Deshima and for two hundred years were the sole contact between Japan and Europe. Through Deshima came a certain amount of Japanese artifacts to the West, mostly porcelain and small pieces of lacquer. Japanese art was thus not entirely unknown in Europe although it was exceeded in quantity by Chinese merchandise with which it was often confused – to untrained Occidental eyes little difference could be seen between the products of the two countries. Although America, Britain and Russia were each for different reasons anxious to take advantage of the entry of Japan into the nineteenth century they were all occupied with wars and it was France under Napoleon III who was able to reap any advantage. French capital was poured into the country to enable the Japanese to build shipyards and iron-foundries and in return Japanese goods were imported into France.

The first examples of Japanese decorative art, prints, netsukes and fousakas (embroidered or printed cloths used in Japan to cover a gift) were of modern manufacture but with a growing knowledge French collectors and connoisseurs became more discriminating. To cater for the demand for older and rarer objects a number of dealers both French and Japanese opened shops in Paris and made trips to the Orient to seek out more important examples. Collections, some of which became the nuclei of museums were in the process of being formed and dealers who had previously specialised in stocking French eighteenth-century furniture and *objets d'art* found it profitable to concentrate wholly or in part on Japanese art.

The profession of *antiquaire* was comparatively recent. Bronzes, paintings and carvings had been collected for centuries through the medium of agents but there had been practically no interest in antique furniture of any period except for pieces which had an association value. During the Gothic revival of the 1830s when the 'style cathédrale' was widespread in France, furniture in the medieval manner was considered preferable to authentic pieces from the Middle Ages. French eighteenth-century furniture was so little esteemed that vast quantities of console-tables, chairs and picture frames which would be priceless today were burnt in the courtyard of Versailles during the Revolution to recover the gold with which they were decorated. Napoleon collected Boulle furniture it is true, but this was exceptional and some of the finest pieces made for Louis XV and Louis XVI found their way to England and other countries outside France. It is generally accepted that the de Goncourt brothers were responsible for a revival of interest in the furniture, porcelain and bibelots of the eighteenth century by their studies and biographies of the period and this awakened interest formed another major influence in Art Nouveau.

The aim of the designers in search of a new style was not so much to plagiarise either the French Rococo or Japanese art as to combine the best qualities of both and to present them in a completely new form suitable to life in the closing years of the nineteenth century and, it was hoped, the twentieth century. This aim was expressed by Geffroy: '... To join together industry and art, to demonstrate that a piece of furniture, a fabric, a light-fitting, a pair of scissors or any object no matter how humble is as worthy of the attention of the artist as a statue or a painting; to elevate all the crafts which employ for decorative purposes line and colour and above all to make our epoch the rival of the eighteenth century and of Japan – to achieve all this has been the aim of the many who are struggling against the decadence of the decorative arts'.

An attempt to reconcile industry and the arts had been made in 1863 (some authorities give the date as 1864) when representatives of various firms connected with the industrial arts joined forces to form 'L'Union Centrale des Beaux-Arts appliqués à l'Industrie'. In 1876, 30,000 francs was endowed to found schools of design in the principal towns outside Paris and three years later 350,000 francs was subscribed for schools of industrial art. These endeavours met with little response and the organisation was on the point of disappearing when in 1880 it was reorganised with different aims. Renamed 'L'Union Centrale des Arts Décoratifs' it was put under the direction of Antonin Proust with the aims of organising exhibitions of decorative arts of all periods with a particular stress on those of the present day and of founding a museum, similar to that at South Kensington which would be a permanent home for the objects accumulated through donations. In 1882 the considerable sum of 6,000,000 francs was raised by a lottery in order to augment the collection and the problem of housing it was solved by the acquisition of the site of a building destroyed in the Commune of 1871. Rodin was commissioned to design an entrance with sculptured figures and called 'La Porte d'Enfer' – rather inappropriate for a museum of decorative art. A change of plans ensued, Rodin's commission was cancelled and in 1904 the collection was installed in the Pavillon Mar-

Figure 5 : Entrance doorway designed by M. L. Leray, c. 1895.

san, a wing of the Louvre, where it found a permanent home. The association was in fact criticised for its failure to follow out the aim expressed in its name, to centralise the decorative arts, and for the hidebound views of its committee which had tended to alienate the artists it was formed to attract and assist.

Antonin Proust was involved in the organisation of the Universal Exhibition of 1889 held to celebrate the hundredth anniversary of the French Revolution. In spite of the abstention of a number of countries, including England, the exhibition was a brilliant success financially and important from an artistic point of view because of the widespread use of advanced techniques of building and the use of iron which was in some cases decorated with ceramic ornaments, not with the intention of disguising the metal structure but of relieving its austerity by the use of glazed and enamelled embellishments. Grouped around the skeletal frame of the Tour d'Eiffel were the Palais des Beaux-Arts, the Palais des Arts Libéraux, the Galerie des Industries with its enormous dome and the Galerie des Machines, all constructed entirely in iron, glass and ceramics.

The Exhibition of 1889 marked the beginning of an extraordinary decade of social history. Politically France was at daggers drawn with England and the old hatred of Germany could never be forgotten while Alsace and parts of Lorraine were still occupied by Germany. It was a decade of colonial expansion when new territories rich in natural products were brought into the sphere of influence of France – notably the island of Madagascar which was brought under French protection. Wealth flowed into the country and Paris was more than ever a city devoted to pleasure, thronged with kings, princes, grand dukes and oriental potentates intent on enjoyment whether they were on state visits or incognito. Women reigned supreme: Sarah Bernhardt and Réjane in the theatre; Loie Fuller dancing at the Folies Bergère; Cléo de Mérode, 'The most beautiful woman in France' dancing at the Ballet de l'Opéra; Yvette Guilbert and Mistinguett the stars of the music-hall; La Goulue, Jane Avril and Anna Held drawing their admirers to Montmartre. In their audiences were often to be seen 'Les Trois Grands' – Emilienne d'Alençon, Liane de Pougy and Caroline Otéro, courtesans who had clawed their way up to the undisputed top of their profession. Their lovers, their fabulous jewels for which, Otéro in particular, they had an insatiable greed, their vast gambling debts, their dresses, hats and automobiles, their horses, and even their perversions were eagerly discussed and such was their flamboyance and vulgarity that Parisians were amused by them and only a few ventured to criticise them on moral grounds. More respectable women were the hostesses of salons held on certain evenings and regular attendance at one of these could further the career of a budding writer, poet or painter. Women were invading the hitherto masculine spheres of poetry, painting, journalism and commerce.

The whole of the Art Nouveau movement was directly involved with this mixture of hedonistic pleasure, tragedies and scandals which rocked the country and divided families. These creative artists were not by force of circumstances dreamy recluses producing beautiful objects far from the distractions of the world; they were practical craftsmen dealing with often tiresome clients on the one hand and with the workmen who executed their designs on the other, for in spite of their extraordinary versatility (Georges de Feure, to name only one from a great many, designed furniture, textiles, porcelain, posters and theatrical costumes in addition to illustrating books) a great deal of their work was actually made by skilled craftsmen working under their supervision.

The period from 1890 to 1900 was one of remarkable activity in the decorative arts in France. So much work was produced that each number of the magazines which sprang up was filled with new examples of furniture textiles and posters, and it is noticeable that after 1903 the number of articles written about *objets d'art* declined and was replaced by those dealing with painters and sculptors, both contemporary and of earlier periods. The output of decorative objects sharply waned as the Art Nouveau style fell out of favour.

The name 'Art Nouveau' was not applied to the new movement until the opening in 1895 of L'Art Nouveau, a shop specialising in modern design, at 22 Rue de Provence by Samuel Bing. By 1900 the term was in general use and can be found even in fashion plates to describe accessories such as jewellery or belt-buckles. It was also used in England in 1896 as a not altogether complimentary name for French decorative art which the English regarded with disfavour as being a style unique to France and having no connection with contemporary work in England. It may be said that Art Nouveau was essentially native to France with little influence from abroad – except, of course, for that of Japanese art. The use of asymmetry borrowed from Japan and Rococo, the absorption in floral or natural forms (even the abstract decorations of scrolls recall the convulations of plant tendrils), the dedication of the style to femininity, and the almost total absence of religious themes differentiate it from the work of the Arts and Crafts movement in England. In this the mystical medievalism of the followers of William Morris is evident, the ornament is strictly symmetrical, the floral decoration highly conventionalised and rigid, the female form on the rare occasions where it appears is draped and virginal, and few objects are made for the adornment of women.

Describing a salon which he had designed for a private house in the Rue Villaret-Joyeuse, the architect Georges Farcy explained that the last vestige of artistic tradition had vanished by the time of the First Empire and that the showy styles of the Renaissance, Louis XV and Louis XVI styles were no longer suitable for modern life which had been so radically altered by scientific discoveries. Consequently he maintained that a new architecture was positively demanded for 'in the first place the rectilinear is only possible as a reminder of the law of gravitation. Objects may be fashioned on the square but every outline that shows visibly on the exterior surface must be full of life and motion so as to delight the eye by its diversity. Symmetrical ornament is out of place in the new art in which every line is supple and winding. The mouldings have been studied with a special view to avoid anything sharp or harsh. There is no straining for outlandish forms; rather the artist's object has been to avoid startling by any exaggeration of detail which is apt to arrest instead of attracting the attention. The colouring of the walls in shades of rose or tenderest green fascinates by its harmonious effect and imparts to the whole a note of warmth far more cheerful than the icy white tone in general vogue. The sight of the soft opalescent tints recalls visions of pale pastels. The new style is one in which Women and Flowers as being typical of all that is freshest and daintiest provide the principal motifs of decoration'. Caprice, a sensuous luxury and an elegance which sometimes sinks to chic are the qualities which distinguish French decorative art in contrast to that of England which was more formal, controlled and austere. Only the aim of allying industry and art was common to both countries – the expression of this aim was completely at variance. Still another difference between the two approaches was that in England a considerable amount of work was anonymous and produced by semi-professionals and amateur artists as can be seen in the pages of *The Studio* which devoted a number of pages to the various competitions which were set each month, the prize winning entries being invariably from amateur sources. The French on the other hand were strictly professional; an object might be hand-made and unique but it was hand-made by a professional with enough pride in craftsmanship to sign the finished article – no French designer would have suffered the rigid anonymity imposed by Liberty's for instance.

It is often mistakenly stated that 'Art Nouveau' as a term was not used in France and that 'Style Moderne' was the name by which the movement was known at the time. This was not the case as an examination of contemporary magazines and periodicals not connected with the arts will show. *Femina* continually mentions Art Nouveau jewellery, Art Nouveau embroideries and has designs for such things as a 'coussin art nouveau'. That the term was in popular use can be seen in *Le Théâtre* for October 1900 where the latest presentation at the Théâtre des Variétés was illustrated. A photograph of one of the tableaux 'L'Art Nouveau à Sèvres' shows Mlle Violette Bichon posing in an attitude taken from Agathon Léonard's biscuit figures exhibited in the Sèvres pavilion at the Universal Exhibition, but whereas the original figure is decorously clad in a long flowing robe with huge frilled sleeves, Mlle Bichon wears only the sleeves, the rest of her appearing to be nude but actually covered from neck to ankles in flesh-coloured silk. Obviously the term 'Art Nouveau' was familiar to the average music hall audience or the point of the tableau would have been lost. A number of writers have repeated the statement that the de Goncourt brothers christened the new decorative idiom 'The Yachting Style' after seeing the Belgian van de Velde's work at L'Art Nouveau Bing and La Maison Moderne, its main competitor. No source is given for this quotation. Jules de Goncourt died in 1870 – van de Velde was seven years old at the time – while Edmond de Goncourt died in 1896, two years before the opening of La Maison Moderne. The opportunities for Edmond de Goncourt's seeing the work of van de Velde are narrowed to the seven months between his visiting Bing's shop on December 30th 1895 and his death in the following July. During that period he regularly made entries in his journal but there is no mention of van de Velde or of any 'Yachting Style'; the only adjective he used in connection with all the furniture at Bing's gallery was 'Anglo-Saxon', not in a complimentary sense. 'Yachting Style' probably refers to something quite different from Art Nouveau – a type of simplified Louis XVI or Directoire style, generally painted white which is to be found as an accessory in the paintings and etchings of Paul Helleu, an ardent yachtsman. His popularity as a portraitist gave weight to his opinions, and furniture and decorations in the style he championed were concurrently fashionable with Art Nouveau and actually superseded it. (A photograph taken in 1903 shows Robert de Montesquiou in his Salon Blanc with its Empire and Directoire furniture arranged formally against Louis XVI panelling and serving as a setting for his portrait by Boldini; the adjoining Salon des Roses was decorated with *treillage* and through a half open door can be seen the famous Japanese collection – relegated to a corridor). For those who could not afford genuine antiques the English firms of Waring and Gillow and Maple, both of whom had branches in Paris, specialised in producing rather spindly versions of Directoire originals with influences of Hepplewhite and Sheraton. Combined with pink striped moiré wallpaper this slightly anaemic style was found to be a flattering background to the dresses of the time, became almost de rigeur for the decorations of hotels and was in fact known irreverently among decorators as 'Louis the Hotel'.

It is impossible to estimate the extent to which the Art Nouveau style was applied to interior decoration not only in Paris but in the provinces as well. With the passing of time many interiors must have vanished and how many still survive in their original form can only be a matter of speculation. Considering how many firms were working at the time in the Art Nouveau manner, apart from the two most celebrated ones L'Art Nouveau Bing and La Maison Moderne, the style

must have been extremely popular in spite of the considerable expense involved. Such a décor with its elaborately involved and intricate decoration of carving could never have been cheap to execute even in its simplest forms as so much hand craftsmanship was necessary. La Maison Moderne was founded in 1898 by the German critic Julius Meier-Graefe with the idea of providing rather less expensive examples of the new art and the socialist Jean Lahor, who translated the works of William Morris into French, founded 'The Society of Popular Art' with the intention of bringing the best of Art Nouveau within the reach of all purses. This venture does not appear to have met with success as nothing further was heard beyond the mention of its foundation.

Art Nouveau found a commercial success by being used to decorate shops, particularly those with a mainly feminine clientèle, and also cafés and restaurants. Few proprietors went so far as one in the provinces who not only decorated his establishment in the most involved type of Art Nouveau but also called it 'Le Café de l'Art Nouveau'. Louis Bigaux decorated Voisin's restaurant in 1898, the dining room of the Hotel Langham was redecorated in 1899, in the same year Maxim's was given the décor which still exists by Louis Marniez and the painter Louis Sonnier, the Brasserie Universelle was redesigned by the Belgian Niermanns in 1902 and the Brasserie Molard was adorned with paintings by Clairin in collaboration with Hippolyte Lucas. Most of the Art Nouveau shopfronts have disappeared but one which was particularly elegant was that for the Magasins des Chocolat Kohler, designed by Plumet in a restrained manner, the simple branching motif of the window supports being continued throughout the interior and combined with yellow and green cloisonné enamel decorative panels.

The nineteenth century was one of the richest in the history of French art where painting was concerned. From David to

Degas, masterpieces were produced which, even if they were not recognised as such and were met with hostility and derision at the time, have since become the prize treasures of museums and collections all over the world. In contrast, the number of sculptors whose work was more than competent is small. Charles Garnier, the architect of the Paris Opera House, chose the sculptors who were to embellish his 'temple of music' with decorative groups from among the most talented of the time – Chapeu, Aizelim, Chabeaud, Evrard, Jean Petit, Aimé Millet, Cabalier, Paul Dubois, Falguière, Barrias, Carrier-Belleuse and Carpeaux. The last-named is remembered mainly for the furore which greeted his 'indecent' group 'La Danse' which was defaced with ink and only saved from removal by the outbreak of the Franco-Prussian War; and Falguière for the scandal surrounding his new statue 'Danseuse' which was recognised as a portrait of Cléo de Mérode, who claimed that her head had been added to the nude body of a professional model. The artistic merits of both works do not seem to have been of any great interest to anyone. But the sculptured figures which can still be seen and judged on the façade of the Paris Opera House are typical examples of the decline of sculpture during the Second Empire.

The rebellion against the academic dictatorship of the Beaux Arts, which was instigated by the Impressionists, had no counterpart among sculptors. Photographs of the big mixed exhibitions of painting and sculpture during the latter half of the century show vast assemblies of gesticulating agitated statues, mainly life-size, interspersed with busts of dignitaries intended for the squares of provincial towns or which after receiving a medal were returned to the artist's studio. The reason why sculptors continued to produce so much work in spite of the high cost of plaster casting, or of the labour of carving in marble, was that there was always a chance that their work might be bought by one of the manufacturers of 'bronzes d'art' and reproduced in a reduced size to supply the constant demand by the public for this type of ornament.

At a time when rooms were crammed with furniture and every table groaned under a load of bric-a-brac, no salon could be considered properly furnished unless it had its quota of bronze statues on marble or onyx bases – the name of the piece and its creator prominently displayed on a metal label. This fashion had started during the latter part of the eighteenth century but at that time the objects were the exquisite terra-cotta statuettes of Clodion, Houdon, or Falconnet, indifferent copies of which were turned out in their thousands during the Second Empire. By the 70s, the firms of Susse, Barbadienne, Denière and Giroux were hard put to execute all the orders they received for castings of bronzes and lesser founders were producing even cheaper versions for less rich and discriminating clients in zinc coloured to look like bronze. Lifesize statues by Falguière and Carpeaux were reduced in scale by the Collas process and often only the head and shoulders of a statue were adapted as small busts as in the case of Falguière's lifesize 'Diana'. Sculpture was 'adapted' as ashtrays, paperweights, paper-knives, the bases of lamps and in particular clock sets, *garnitures de cheminées* consisting of a clock flanked by a pair of candlesticks or ornamental urns. Inevitably sculptors began creating original models for these objects, particularly so in the Art Nouveau manner when the desire was that a similar feeling should pervade all the contents of a room.

The two most outstanding sculptors working in the Art Nouveau circle were probably Alexandre Charpentier whose medals will be referred to later, and Jean Dampt. Both attempted with varying success to combine sculpture and furniture design. Dampt in particular was emphatic in his views that no recourse should be made to past styles in creating works of art in 1900 – views which in practice he ignored, for much of his work has obvious German Gothic inspiration. Rupert Carabin besides modelling small bronzes of rather gauche figures of dancers, created a number of pieces of furniture which combine practicability with eroticism. Nude female figures in almost lifesize half-relief support or clamber over upright pianos, chairs, tables and vitrines, often accompanied by Persian cats. His work reflects the current interest in the mild pornography of Felicien Rops, the early novels of Willy and erotic Japanese prints.

Painters and poets alike fell under the spell of the dancer Loie Fuller after her début in 1893, and endeavoured to portray the movement and colour of her performances on canvas and in verse; sculptors, too, were fascinated by the shapes made by her fluttering draperies in which the figure of the dancer was half seen or completely disappeared. Two sculptors in particular produced a number of versions of La Loie's dancing. Raoul Larche is now known mainly for his statuettes in gilded bronze of the dancer – statuettes which often incorporate a small electric bulb hidden in the draperies, giving a mysterious light and an effect of movement (plate 22). Pierre Roche, trained as a painter in the studio of Roll, turned to sculpture on the advice of Dalou, whose terra-cotta portrait busts and groups were in great demand, particularly by the English Royal Family. As in the case of Larche, Roche is now best remembered for his statues and portrait heads of Loie Fuller, and for his sculptures for the charming temporary theatre designed for her by Henri Sauvage as a setting for her performances in the 1900 Paris Exhibition. The façade was entirely sculptured in the form of draperies flowing from two lifesize figures of the dancer which flanked the entrance, while the range of small windows in the eaves was interspersed with portrait masks of Loie Fuller.

The last quarter of the nineteenth century witnessed a revival of the art of the medallist which had been neglected since the time of the first Napoleon. The invention of a mechanical process by means of which a large relief could be reduced to a very much smaller size, accurately reproducing the design in miniature without any loss of detail, thus saving a great deal of minute work and consequent eyestrain, had encouraged sculptors to take a renewed interest in this neglected art. In 1895, the decision was taken to change the coinage of France which had remained unaltered since the 1848 Republic. The old designs of Dupré and Oudine were felt to be unsuitable to the spirit of the Third Republic and through the efforts of Roger Marx, the acknowledged expert on history of medals, the designs for the gold coins were entrusted to Chaplain, recently appointed a director of the Sèvres factory, those for the silver coins to Roty, while Dupuis was entrusted with the bronze coins. This long overdue step, combined with the action of the State in commissioning artists to submit designs for commemorative medals which could be acquired by collectors, led to the formation of the 'Société des Amis de la Medaille', the object of which was to issue to its members medals which were to be specially designed and cast in editions limited to the numbers of subscribers, thus ensuring a rarity value.

Oscar Roty was one of the first sculptors to have interested himself in the revival and was responsible for the introduction of medals which were square or rectangular, sometimes with a curved top. He also abandoned the general custom of confining the lettering to the edge of the medal and incorporated it in the general design; another innovation for which he was responsible was the creation of decorative medallions which could be mounted as brooches or pendants. These proved so popular that his example was followed by Bernon, Victor Prouvé (Gallé's collaborator at Nancy) and Ovide Yencesse. Chaplain's work had a boldness and strength which ensured their demand by collectors; his finely modelled portrait plaques, in particular that of Charles Garnier, have dignity combined with a delineation of character conveyed by the subtle modelling. An early death cut short the promising career of Daniel Dupuis – two commemorative medals of his were struck in the presence of visitors to the Paris Exhibition and no fewer than 50,000 impressions were sold.

In 1893 the Paris Mint took a further step in inaugurating the practice of commissioning designs for medals which had no particular commemorative significance and this recognition of the medal purely as a work of art with a wider area of subject matter not only encouraged sculptors but also had a practical result in proving the source of a new income to the Mint.

It was in this circumstance of a renewed interest that the greatest exponent found recognition. Alexandre Charpentier was born in extremely humble circumstances but soon showed a natural aptitude for modelling in clay. Unfortunately, the fees for the sculpture classes were more than he could possibly afford and so as a second best he enrolled at a school of medal engraving, the fees being considerably lower. He was so poor that after paying fees his he had no money left for a lodging and was reduced to sleeping under the bridges of Paris in the company of the clochards. The lack of a conventional training in sculpture in three dimensions was no impediment to Charpentier, who may have benefited from not being forced to follow the ideals of classic sculpture which were still rigidly enforced in the orthodox sculpture classes. His predecessors for the most part used hard well-defined outlines and chiselled effects.

Charpentier's medals are characterised by their soft, almost molten appearance, combined with a strength of design and the replacement of idealised classical figures by more naturalistic ones. Limiting himself in general to a very low relief, he succeeded in suggesting depth by daring foreshortening and the device of continuing the inscription behind the figure in such an ingenious manner that it is still completely legible in spite of being partly obscured. His exquisite medallions

were eagerly sought after by collectors and their popularity led to his being asked to design door furniture and fingerplates by the firm of Fontaine – Charpentier supplied original models for these and they were reproduced commercially (plate 25).

Intrigued by some Japanese examples which had been brought to his notice, he succeeded in mastering the technique of *papier gauffré* by means of which a relief can be impressed on paper which had been dampened and pressed on a matrix. Charpentier after long experiments discovered that a matrix could be made of a number of layers of cigarette paper which was flexible enough for the embossed paper to be removed without damage. These were at first produced as small decorative panels for framing, such as his portrait of Edmond de Goncourt, with the added advantage that they were both lighter and cheaper to produce than metal medallions. He was soon asked to produce *gauffré* letter headings for commercial firms. A similar technique was used to impress reliefs on leather bindings – except that in this case a metal matrix was used – and these were employed by publishing firms to place their house-mark on the imitation leather wrappers which protected paper-bound volumes of limited editions of illustrated books such as *Ilsée, Princesse de Tripoli* by Robert de Fleurs which was decorated by Alphonse Mucha.

The art of bookbinding had remained stubbornly faithful to the standards and, in most cases, the designs originated in the seventeenth and eighteenth centuries which were regarded as a peak of achievement; the great binders of the beginning of the nineteenth century added to the repertoire of designs with their bindings in the Gothic manner – generally known as 'le style cathédrale' – but they remained constant to the rules governing the disposition of ornament which had previously lain down the spine of the book in panels of small designs, the front and back covers of a strictly symmetrical

Figure 6 : Bookbinding by René Weimer, *c.* 1895.

arrangement with a border of ornament and a central motif. Variety might be introduced by means of inlays of leather of different colours, but the ornament was restricted to the use of tooling, either gilded or blind. It was considered essential that new editions should harmonise with an already existing collection of fine bindings. In 1880 Amand produced bindings which broke with tradition and which were admired and collected by critics such as Edmond de Goncourt and Octave Uzanne but an early death prevented his work becoming sufficiently well-known to have any great influence. However, the growing use of coloured lithography for printing the covers of paper-bound books had an influence on the binders of de luxe editions, and of single volumes printed for private libraries. The interest in Japanese art, its two-dimensional decorative effects and its disregard of Western principles of perspective, also had an influence on an art in which a design is carried out in flat areas of coloured leather. Painters were commissioned to decorate plain vellum binding with drawings in water colour or with pen and washed sketches – Eugène Grasset's decorations for *L'Eloge de la Folie* and Raffaelli's for *Les Types de Paris*, are examples of this, while others were executed by Renoir, Willete, Morin and Henriot. Pierre Roche created *reliures eglomisés* – semi-transparent vellum painted on the back before being stuck on the covers – thus giving the effect of translucent enamels.

These bindings were criticised when exhibited as being unorthodox, neither paintings nor bookbindings. The complete break with traditional ornament, though not with the classic technique of bookbinding, came with the work of a number of binders and designers of the Nancy School, headed by Camille Martin, whose work was continued after his early death by Victor Prouvé, René Weimer, Antoinette Vallgran and Madame Waldeck-Rousseau, all of whom produced bindings of a type which had never been seen before. Prouvé designed bindings which had a close resemblance to the inlaid panels in furniture by Emil Gallé, with whom he worked a great deal. Weimer, a protégé of Prouvé, first exhibited a collection of bindings in 1893 and soon attracted attention by the richness and variety of his covers for books such as Pierre Louys's *Aphrodite*, decorated with the objects which led to the downfall of the courtesan heroine of this erotic novel set in ancient Alexandria. A volume on Jean Carriès, the potter, has a conventionalised decoration similar to the white glaze on a coloured ground with which Carriès embellished vases, combined with a metal portrait head in low relief. Several of Prouvé's bindings incorporated metal plaques as in Roger Marx's *La Medaille* and *Les Chauves Souris* decorated with flying bats in iron, while another volume incorporated a large metal crab on the front cover.

The rigid symmetry and the delicate lace-like effect of gilded floral motifs were abandoned in favour of a bold asymmetrical design which, in many cases, was not confined to the front cover but spread all over the front, spine and back of the book, often justifying the criticism that in order to see the full effect of the design the book must be held in an unnatural position and that the use of metal plaques as decoration prevented the volumes being placed in bookcases unless their neighbours were to be damaged. Justified as these criticisms might be, the important fact is that the design of bookbinding was revolutionised and a fine binding began to be regarded as a creative work of art.

The Japanese influence can be seen in the work of Georges Auriol who produced a volume *Le Livre des Monogrammes, Marques, Cachets et ex Libris* in 1892, which was followed by a second collection published seven years later with a foreword by that indefatigable writer of prefaces, Anatole France. Each book contained reproductions of some five hundred monograms Auriol had designed for friends or business firms, ranging from Madame Cheruit, the dressmaker, to Messrs Cadburys, whose device was still used until very recently.

In an area of less than an inch in diameter he contrived to produce a design which was elegant, simple and at the same time immediately legible.

The last quarter of the nineteenth century witnessed the development of the sumptuously produced book not only elaborately bound but also illustrated by celebrated artists and issued in a small edition. These limited editions were eagerly subscribed for and a few months after publication a volume could easily change hands at several times its original cost. Naturally not all of these volumes were of a high quality of design or execution but the interest they aroused gave an impetus to the illustration of books in colour which was furthered by the development of new printing techniques.

Eugène Grasset, a naturalised Frenchman of Swiss birth, had been from an early age interested in the study of architecture and had designed wallpapers and textiles but it was his experiments in typography which first attracted the attention of the publisher Charles Gillot, who, in 1881, encouraged him to design the type and to produce illustrations for the *Histoire des Quatre Fils Aymon*, a collection of medieval legends and fables. In two years the work was ready for publication; conceived in a manner which anticipated the Art Nouveau style, the layout and illustrations show a variety of influences from Japanese prints to the drawings of Gustave Doré, combined with a precise and archeologically-correct rendering of medieval ornament. Grasset's water colour drawings were faithfully reproduced by the chrome-lithographic process, but in spite of the care taken in its production the volume was received with indifference by the general public until the critic Octave Uzanne wrote an article praising it in *Le Livre*, a periodical devoted to the art of the book. Grasset later designed a number of type faces, notably that used by Meier-Graefe in the publications associated with the latter's shop La Maison Moderne. Incidentally, it is surprising how many volumes of this period were still using types dating from the 40s and 50s, even in the case of the volume of poems *Le Chef des Odeurs Suaves*, where one would have expected the author Robert de Montesquiou, usually so concerned about matters of taste, to have wanted a more modern type face.

The eventual success of Grasset's volume led to many other books being produced in a similar manner. Carlos Schwabe illustrated Baudelaire's *Les Fleurs du Mal* with coloured etchings in a volume bound by Charles Meunier, and with coloured pen and ink drawings to illustrate *L'Evangile de l'Enfance de N. S. Jésus-Christ*. Gaston de Latenaye's delicate drawings adorned *Nausikaa* while Boutet de Monval decorated *Nos Enfants* and *Chansons de France*. Albums of drawings in pen and ink were published of the work of Willette, Steinlen, Forain and the humorous drawings of Caran d'Ache – a Frenchman named Jean Poirier who used the pseudonym taken from the Russian name 'karandash' for a pencil.

The malaise afflicting other forms of decorative art had also shown itself in the products of the Sèvres factory which held a virtual monopoly of the manufacture of pottery and porcelain in the nineteenth century. The high technical quality of modelling, painting and gilding which had been reached during the Consulate and Empire periods, when the somewhat frigid Neo-Classical taste of the architects Percier and Fontaine imposed itself on all the decorative arts, was not maintained under the succeeding regime after 1815. The standard of painting soon degenerated, the subtle rose and blue grounds of the eighteenth century became garish to please a less cultivated clièntele, the forms became either clumsy versions of earlier models or were overburdened with meaningless ornament. A series of uninspired directors had brought the reputation of the Sèvres factory to a low ebb by 1851 when the French exhibit at the Great Exhibition was severely criticised both at home and abroad.

The revival of French ceramic art was due to Ernest Chaplet, who had entered the Sèvres factory in 1848 as a boy of thirteen; after training there for some years he left to join the Lavrin factory at Bourg-le-Reine, a very much smaller establishment but one which gave him greater opportunities for exercising his ability. The over-elaborate 'period' decorations so much in favour had no appeal for Chaplet, who found his inspiration in the *flambé* glazes combined with the simple forms of the Chinese potters and after long efforts he succeeded in approximating the richness and depth of the Chinese glazes, gradually extending his range from the copper reds to grey-violet, blue and white.

Jean Carriès, a generation younger than Chaplet, was more influenced by Japanese pottery and in particular by the simpler pieces associated with the tea ceremony which were beginning to make their appearance in Europe in the 1870s; the first exports from Japan had been of either contemporary pottery and porcelain or products made expressly for the European market, and it was not for some years that a more severe type of pottery esteemed by Japanese connoisseurs found its way to Europe. These intensely individual pieces were of more interest to a potter with his own kiln than to a factory such as Sèvres, where the production of large numbers of identical pieces was essential for commercial usage. Carriès had started his career as a sculptor, and in consequence when he devoted himself to pottery he found it natural to model strange animal figures in addition to the pots which he covered in thick richly-coloured glazes, often accentuated with flecks of gold. His career was cut short by his death in 1894 at the early age of thirty-nine, and although he left behind a body of work which was highly praised, his imitators brought his ideas into disrepute, lacking the fastidious taste and sure touch of the originator.

Chaplet's pupil August Delaherche was another artist who respected his craft and refused to pander to popular taste.

His work was first exhibited at an exhibition in 1889, and the simple, strong shapes of his vases aroused great admiration. Seeking only what he conceived to be perfection, he would ruthlessly destroy a vase which he did not consider worthy to bear his signature. Like Carriès, he was greatly influenced by Japanese pottery and relied for effect upon the beauty of coloured glaze rather than on decoration, though on occasion he would ornament a vase with a simple floral motif incised in the clay before it was glazed. Together with Jean Dalpayrat, another pupil of Chaplet, he founded a school of pottery 'L'Art du Feu'.

The success of these independent potters and the favourable notices which their work received when it was shown at exhibitions, proved a stimulus to the Sèvres factory. In order to introduce new ideas, artists and sculptors who had not had any training in ceramics were brought into the factory and for two years – from 1880 to 1882 – Rodin was engaged as a modeller (plate 31). In 1884 a process which had been discovered by the chemist Ebelmann during the Second Empire, and which had been neglected, was revived by the technical director of the factory, Vogt. Known by the splendid title of 'Porcelaine avec Couverte de Crystallisation Grand Feu de Four', it was a process of glazing on a white biscuit by means of which the effect of three-dimensional crystals in pastel tones of violet, mauve and green, was obtained (plate 7). Large vases in this technique were included in the Sèvres exhibit at the 1900 Exhibition. New models of figurines of various sizes and subjects were commissioned from the sculptor Joseph Chéret, brother of Jules Chéret. Models of animals were realised from sculptures by Gardet, and Théodore Rivière's 'Phryné' had a success at the 1900 Exhibition rivalling that of Agathon Léonard's 'La Danse de l'Echarpe', a set of figures of Greek dancers intended to serve as a decoration for a dining table (plate 22). Produced as prestige pieces for exhibitions were the vases of imposing size ranging from three to five feet in height, and of shapes named 'Clagny', 'Auxerre' and 'Dijon', which were for sale at high prices from five to ten thousand francs. They were painted by the resident artists Bienville, Gebleux and Fournier with subjects such as 'La Mer' or 'La Terre' with a strong resemblance to the decoration found on Japanese Satsuma ware, still being produced at that time.

The technical innovations of Chaplet and Carriès were carried on by numerous individual potters; such as Jean Dalpayrat, whose smaller pieces were enhanced with metal mounts by Maurice Dufrêne and were sold at La Maison Moderne in the Rue des Petits Champs; Bigot, whose vases with a dull glaze were similarly decorated with silver and pewter mounts designed by Henri van de Velde; Edmond Lachenal, who specialised in making vases in the form of flowers with a strong Japanese feeling (plate 27), and who invented the *email velouté* finish, obtained by immersing the finished vase in a tin of acid which gave the glaze a velvety surface; Taxile Doat, said to be an Englishman in spite of his exotic name, employed at the Sèvres factory (plate 30) but later set up on his own and specialised in white glazes; Henri de Vallombreuse whose small vases with thick irregular encrustation of white glaze on a dark ground, gave the appearance of being half-covered in snow and Decœur, noted for the simplicity of his vases, combined with rich red or green glazes, and for his white glaze speckled with black (plate 30). Clément-Massier established a factory at Golfe-st-Juan and perfected an iridescent glaze, mainly peacock blue or emerald green in colour, with which he covered pots and decorative plaques; although he consciously adopted the forms of Greek and Roman vases, his glaze was not an imitation of the iridescence of antique glass but was based on the metallic lustres of Hispano-Moresque pottery. For some time Clément-Massier collaborated with Lévy-Dhurmer, one of the few painters whose work was influenced by Art Nouveau, and the decorations on pottery by Clément-Massier are probably his work (plates 28, 29).

Albert Dammouse, son of a sculptor employed at Sèvres, was taught by Chaplet and in 1892 founded his own kiln at Sèvres. There he perfected an intricate technique of applying a porcelain decoration modelled as flowers or fruit on a pottery base. The porcelain gave it greater freedom of detail but presented difficulties in firing the combination of two materials at the same time. Towards 1900 he created small cups and vessels of paper thinness with a matt glaze; these closely resembled the *pâte de verre* which Henri Cros was perfecting at the Sèvres factory. Cros is credited with the invention in the 70s of this technique of firing ground glass in a mould producing an effect of sculpture in coloured wax or tinted alabaster. His work was continued after his death by his son Jean Cros, and imitated by François Decorchement, Almeric Walter, who worked at the Daum factory at Nancy, and by Argy-Rousseau who created plaques decorated with floral motifs for use as jewellery in addition to small exquisite vases and bowls (plate 36).

In discussing glass of this period there is one name which is not only pre-eminent in this field but which is almost synonymous with Art Nouveau – that of Emil Gallé. By sheer artistry of technique and fertility of imagination, his finest works, whether produced by him personally or under his close supervision, entitle him to be considered as one of the great artists in glass of any period. His father, Charles Gallé, owned a glass factory in Nancy, the capital of the former Duchy of Lorraine, where a tradition of fine glass-making had survived since the sixteenth century. Emil Gallé was sent at an early age to Weimar and Meisenthal for training before joining the family business. Even as a child, Gallé had a passionate interest in botany which was to last his whole life; his desire to create new effects in glass necessitated his learning chemistry and the use of rare metals to obtain the subtle colours he needed to interpret the beauties of nature. His contribution to the Exhibition 'La Terre, la Pierre et le Verre' at the Palais d'Industrie in 1884 attracted considerable attention; at this period he was using a clear glass, either lightly tinted in a pale brown or a dark green with enamelled decoration of flowers and insects in the Japanese manner, the ground of the design often being acid-etched in a design both inside and outside the vase (plate 33). In 1889 he began to experiment with opaque and coloured glass with enamel decorations, showing a greater freedom of imagination in the shape and ornament; from 1897 onwards the colours grew more subtle and the texture of the glass more milky and opalescent, though an experiment in creating black and white glass proved unpopular. The decorations of his vases were taken from nature, either flowers – even pre-historic forms reflecting his interest in palaeontology – or insects, particularly the dragonfly, *la libellule*, an insect dear to the designers of the period. His technique of superimposing several layers of differently tinted glass, which were then cut away by grinding or by acid to reveal the design in the different shades of colour, were said to have been inspired by Chinese snuff bottles (plate 34). Many of his earlier vases were created to illustrate a theme and incorporated into the designs are lines or phrases taken from poems by Victor Hugo, Verlaine, Anna de Noailles, and by his friend and patron Robert de Montesquiou. Gallé, in common with a number of his contemporaries, was convinced that nature and the forms of plants, fruits and flowers, should be a basis for a new school of design, which would dispel the curse of historicism which had afflicted the decorative arts for so long, and above his studio door he had inscribed the words:

    'Our roots are deep in the woods

    Among the mosses, close to the springs.'

which were inspired by a phrase of Moleschott: 'It is the plants that bind us to the earth; they are our roots'.

Gallé's fame and genius tend to overshadow the work of the brothers Auguste and Antonin Daum who, assisted by Jean Gruber, created many finely conceived and executed pieces from 1890 onwards in a style which was influenced by Gallé to a great extent (plates 33, 34). They were associated with him in the 'Ecole de Nancy', which he formed in 1901, an association of the various designers centred at Nancy formed to hold exhibitions of their work.

There was of course a considerable amount of glass produced by other firms in the current manner, but for the most part it was inferior in every way to that produced at Nancy. The standard of workmanship is generally low and usually indicantes a desire to capitalise on the fashion rather than to be a genuine creative expression.

As the designers of Art Nouveau aimed to make every object harmonise with femininity, it is hardly surprising to find that jewellery design reached a high point during this period. René Lalique revolutionised jewellery design with his first exhibition in 1894. He introduced polychromatic jewellery to take the place of the heavy diamond pieces which had been in vogue since the opening up of the mines in South Africa. He used not only coloured precious stones but also the humbler semiprecious ones and even carved glass, either coloured or iridescent and opaque. His designs were highly imaginative and employed stylised versions of natural flora and insect forms. One of his innovations was to use carved horn, mainly for hair combs which were necessary for the elaborate hairstyles of the time. This was beautifully and naturalistically carved as pansies or autumn sycamore leaves and then enhanced by a scattering of diamond dew or small gold insects.

Lalique's first concern was to make jewellery a work of art in its own right and a decorative adjunct, rather than a display of wealth. Luckily the exquisite workmanship and subtle colouring of his examples met with immediate success and Sarah Bernhardt became his most famous patron. He became a Chevalier of the Légion d'Honneur three years after his first exhibition and in 1900 found all his work at the Paris Exposition bought by the millionaire Gulbenkian. Shortly after this he turned successfully to glass making. None of the masses of cheaper jewellery which was turned out in the Art Nouveau period can be ranked with his work (plates 39, 40), comparable only with that of Fabergé, his contemporary in Russia.

The invention of lithography at the end of the eighteenth century greatly increased the range of advertising, which until then had been confined to the use of printed posters illustrated with wood blocks laboriously coloured by hand. By 1860 the technical difficulties of printing in one or more colours had been overcome, and the advantages of using highly coloured posters were fully realised in spite of the increase in cost. It was not until 1866 when Jules Chéret, 'the father of the pictorial poster', returned to Paris at the age of thirty from London, where he had been learning the latest techniques of colour lithography, and started a printing establishment where every coloured poster of any merit was seen, although his work at this period lacked the distinction it acquired in later years. His technique of drawing on the lithographic stone in pen and ink and limiting his colours to red, blue and yellow, gave an effect of heaviness. In 1878 he abandoned the use of pen and ink for crayon, the softer outline lending a lightness to the drawing. From 1890 he favoured a blue outline, which contributed a more brilliant effect and a trip to Spain in the following year further lightened his palette, the brilliant sunlight and vivid colours having made a great impression on him. By now he was established as the foremost poster designer of the day, and his Columbines, Pierrots and Shepherdesses (inspired by Watteau and other eighteenth-century artists) were to be found all over Paris and indeed all France, not only on the outside of buildings or on hoardings but inside as well, for the public were finding them so attractive that they were being used as decorations for rooms, to an extent that the manufacturers of the wallpapers began to be seriously concerned.

Indeed the popularity of his colourful and high-spirited work had started a fashion for collecting posters about 1875. Agencies were set up in London, Paris and later New York, where copies of posters by Chéret and other artists could be obtained, and magazines such as *The Poster* in England, a similarly named publication in New York, which unfortunately lasted for only three issues, and *L'Estampe et L'Affiche* in Paris, gave collectors the latest developments in poster art. However, the demand for larger posters and numerically greater editions was hampered by the limitations of lithographic printing from stone blocks which were not only heavy and cumbrous to handle but were easily damaged and required enormous storage space. The development of the refining of aluminium for commercial purposes led to the invention of 'Algraphy', by means of which a sheet of aluminum was substituted for a stone block. Substantially, the same effects could be obtained with the added advantage of a greater number of impressions – up to 100,000 if necessary – without the plates showing signs of wear and the flexibility of the aluminium enabled them to be wrapped round the cylinder for rotary printing while their thinness required far less storage space.

Chéret's first rival in popularity was the Swiss-born artist Eugène Grasset. As we have seen earlier, he had made an intensive study of medieval art, and also of the Japanese masters of the colour print, and elements of these diverse influences can be found in all his work. Before long, his dreamy maidens reminiscent of those of Botticelli, usually red-haired and dressed in long, full, flowered robes were advertising beer, ink and chocolate, on every hoarding. They were widely imitated, ineptly by Paul Berthon, and with more

success by Verneuil, Donnay and the Belgian Berchmanns. However, his use of a thick outline gives a static quality to his posters, far removed from the exuberance of those of Chéret, and it is not surprising that Sarah Bernhardt was not pleased with his poster for the production of *Jeanne d'Arc* in 1894, for the medieval atmosphere of the play is stressed at the expense of the personal attractions of Madame Bernhardt.

Bernhardt first used the work of Alphonse Mucha in this year, when his design for a poster for her new production of *Ghismonda* was presented to her, and it was the appearance of this poster which led not only to his being placed under contract to the actress for a number of years, but also to his recognition as a new and dynamic influence on the growing interest in Art Nouveau. It was followed by a series featuring the flamboyant star, *La Tosca, Lorenzaccio, La Dame Aux Camélias, Medée, Hamlet* and *La Samaritaine*, which have since become collectors' items, as eagerly sought after now as they were at the time. Mucha's use of areas of flat colour enclosed in strong lines was more successful than Grasset's use of the same elements, but his love of fantastically patterned wreaths of hair and of subtle colours, often combined with gold or silver, gave rise to criticism that though his posters might be a delight to the eye at close quarters, they had difficulty in withstanding the competition of more strident neighbours. Nevertheless, the success of his theatrical posters led to his being commissioned by business firms and for the next few years Parisians were admiring and collecting Mucha's designs for products from bicycles – the 90s saw a rage for bicycling – to cigarette papers and beer (plate 46).

The many modern reproductions of the posters of Toulouse-Lautrec have tended to over-familiarise our eyes with them and it is difficult to realise the impact they must have had when they were first shown. A contemporary writer commented 'The obvious word for Lautrec's work is – unhealthy'. But he admitted that 'If the placards of Chéret dance in disordered joy on the hoardings and thus arrest our attention, if those of Mucha catch the eye from sheer extravagance and decoration, those of Lautrec inevitably bring one to a standstill and retain one until the significance of the legend has been mastered.' Lautrec depicted the dancers and entertainers of the Montmartre district with a 'terrible reality' but he never passed judgment on the characters he portrayed with such evil elegance and with a personal vision at once ruthless and factual. His posters were directly related to the contemporary scene and were not originally intended as decorative statements which happened to advertise certain products and entertainments.

Equally realistic were the posters of Steinlen and Moreau-Nélaton; the former's poster for the printing firm of Charles Verneau depicted a frieze of types who were part of the everyday life of the streets of Paris, washerwomen, nurse-maids, workmen, elegant ladies, midinettes and children. A poster for sterilised milk shows Steinlen at his most tender and charming – a small girl, red-headed and wearing a red dress, sips a bowl of milk greedily watched by three of the cats Steinlen loved so much – a composition arresting to the eye and yet in spite of its subject treated without a trace of sentimentality. Georges de Feure, whose work receives less than due credit, was with Orazi a designer of the decorative school. Both men produced only a limited number of posters but de Feure's *Isita* and his *A Jeanne d'Arc* (for a provincial fabric store) are among the finest of the period. The latter of the tall rectangular shape taken from Japanese kakemonos is in tones of brown and gold and shows a full-length figure of the saint in fantastic armour and wearing her hair in the style favoured by the famous beauty Cléo de Mérode; the poster is dated 1896, the year Mademoiselle won the first beauty competition ever organised.

Some of the established painters essayed poster design, usually on behalf of an exhibition of either their own work

Figure 7 : Poster by Pierre Bonnard, 1892.

or that of a friend. Eugène Carrière executed a portrait of Rodin in the sombre heavily-shadowed style which had brought him fame and a reputation of being one of the glories of contemporary French art; Puvis de Chavannes, advanced in years and venerated as the greatest living painter, was not, unfortunately, happy in the medium and his conception for the centenary of the invention of lithography in 1895 cannot be considered successful. Bonnard's poster for the 'Salon des Cent' of 1896 was printed by Chéret's firm and is a delight in its wit and elegance. Willette, Malteste, Bottini, Misti, Pal, Roedel, Réalier-Dumas, Grün — the list of designers whose work enlivened the streets is endless but for the most part their designs were either mediocre or derivative. The number of posters produced suggests that advertising must have been a profitable business for all concerned.

A collection of posters naturally needed sufficient wall space to display them adequately, but the collection of pictorial postcards was an easier matter. These were produced in vast quantities and at least two periodicals were published specialising in information about the new issues of illustrated postcards. Mucha found a new public and a new source of income when his posters were reproduced in miniature without any lettering on postcards and he designed a set of cards representing the months of the year. Photographs of actresses and dancers, often with a decorative background in the Art Nouveau manner, were sold by the thousand, the most popular being portraits of Cléo de Mérode (plate 14). Much admired were the floating nymphs of Mastroanni which continued to be popular up to the 1914 war.

The 1900 Exhibition was at once the apogee and the finale of Art Nouveau. In spite of the efforts of Julius Meier-Graefe and his colleagues at La Maison Moderne, opened two years before the Exhibition, the influence of the 'new art' had been limited to a comparatively small circle of well-to-do people who could afford the high prices of individually created objects or of examples produced in small limited editions. Popularised and brought to the attention of a wider circle, Art Nouveau very soon began to be produced in far larger quantities with a consequent deterioration in the standards of design. Intent only on turning out large quantities of objects in the current fashion and in making them as cheaply as possible, manufacturers cut down their initial expenses by dispensing with designers altogether and producing cheapened version of existing work. The cycle had been completed and the very thing that Art Nouveau had been intended to combat overtook Art Nouveau itself. Dismayed by the vulgarisation of their work the more talented designers began to experiment in other directions. Two of the most influential figures, Bing in Paris and Gallé in Nancy disappeared from the scene. Bing retired in 1902 and L'Art Nouveau once more became a gallery of Far Eastern art and antiquities while Gallé, the mainstay of the Ecole de Nancy, died in 1904.

By 1905 the movement had to all intents and purposes finished though echoes of the original style survived until about 1914. New influences were on the way. Oriental trends inspired by the Arabian Nights Entertainment had already appeared in 1900 and under the aegis of young designers such as Paul Poiret these were to grow into the exoticisms of dress and interior decoration which culminated in Bakst's designs for the ballet *Scheherazade*. Collectors were beginning to feel the attraction not unmixed with repulsion of African art. Fashion, changing more rapidly than ever before with the quickening pace of events and helped by the new techniques of reproduction in magazines and newspapers, abandoned the pale flowers and the sinuous curves, for richer harmonies and more rigid and geometrical forms. But short-lived as Art Nouveau was, it had served its purpose. It had demonstrated that it was not necessary to pillage from past styles in creating a new one and that fine quality in design and craftsmanship could go hand in hand with experiment.

Notes on the illustrations

BLACK AND WHITE ILLUSTRATIONS

Figure 1 and **2** Frontispiece *Interior details from Le Printemps* by Sédille. 1880.
The model for innumerable department stores in France, England, America and Germany was Le Printemps built to the designs of Sédille and opened in 1880. Situated on a site adjoining the Rue de Provence (where Bing's L'Art Nouveau was later opened) the exterior elevations of iron and glass were revolutionary in that they indicated the disposition of the interior elements in a composition of strongly marked verticals broken by glass bays providing an unusual amount of lighting. The main feature of the interior was the central hall extending the whole height of the building with massive pillars supporting an elaborately shaped glass roof. The various floors of the store were open on to this central court from which they derived light and ventilation as well as from the exterior windows. The balustrade of the main staircase, which was the central feature of the main hall, was as original in its treatment as the rest of the building, its conventional floral decoration leading the eye to the upper floors. Stylistically the wrought iron ornaments resemble the designs of Viollet-le-Duc. A less ambitious version of this concept was to be found in Whiteley's Stores in Queensway with a similar but simpler staircase.

Figure 3 Frontispiece *Entrance to the Paris Exhibition.* 1900.
The great archway, flanked by two obelisks, was decorated with glazed earthenware by Bigot and studded with coloured electric light bulbs; the base included two long horizontal panels 'Le Travail' also in earthenware by Emile Müller from the original models by Guillot. Moreau-Vauthier in collaboration with the architect Binet decided that an allegorical 'Fame' or 'Glory' in the classic manner would not be representative of the purpose of the Exhibition and that a figure in modern dress would more fittingly welcome visitors and, incidentally, the new century. The result, 'La Parisienne', a colossal figure of a woman wearing a semi-stylised version of contemporary fashion, caused more admiration and derision than any of the hundreds of more conventional statues which decorated every available space in the Exhibition.

Figure 4 *Designs for Métro entrances* by Hector Guimard. 1900.
A competition was held for designs for the Paris Métro stations and although Hector Guimard was not placed first his designs for the entrances were preferred to those of the first prize winner. Examples of the entrances shown here, of glass, iron and decorated panels, were erected all over Paris except in the Place de l'Opéra where a more conventional design was used. The ironwork and all the details were based on natural plant forms. Unfortunately most of the entrances have now been removed owing to iron deterioration.

Figure 5 *Entrance doorway* by M. L. Leray. *c.* 1895.
This doorway with its flat-headed Louis XV arch is in the Rue Bezout. The exaggerated keystone and sculptured flower decoration appear on many houses of this period and continued to be popular until 1914. In this case the flower motif is a thistle which is the patriotic flower of Lorraine whose capital, Nancy, was the home of so many Art Nouveau designers. The recent compulsory cleaning of Parisian buildings has revealed many examples of this motif. The gate itself uses wrought-iron for free asymmetrical ornamentation.

Figure 6 *Bookbinding* by René Weimer. *c.* 1895.
An exhibition of modern bookbindings was held at Bing's L'Art Nouveau in 1896 and the one shown here was exhibited in it. It makes use of inlaid coloured leather tooled in gold. The asymmetry and conventionalized flowers in the design are typical of the period and can be seen echoed in the work of Mucha and de Feure.

Figure 7 *Poster* by Pierre Bonnard, 1892.
This advertisement for champagne was the first poster which Bonnard carried out and he was obviously influenced by the frolicsome art of Jules Chéret. His vitality contrasts with the more static approach of Mucha and Grasset.

THE PLATES

Plate 1 *Dining room from a house in Paris.* Designed by Collet and with paintings by Lucien Lévy-Dhurmer. 1910. Metropolitan Museum of Art, New York. Harris Brisbane Dick Fund, 1966.
A late example of Art Nouveau when the linear elements were losing ground to an encrustation of naturalistically rendered floral decoration. This type of ornament can be seen on the exterior of many buildings in Paris dating from an early example, the Hôtel Lutetia in 1900, to a number of private houses or small apartment blocks which the recent cleaning of the façades have revealed as bearing dates ranging up to 1914. The pale luminous paintings are in Lévy-Dhurmer's later style.

A considerable number of rooms of this type, with or without mural paintings must have been created between 1890 and 1905, most of which have disappeared with changes in fashion and especially during the 1920s when Art Nouveau was regarded with disfavour. Some twenty important decorators exhibited rooms in the Art Nouveau manner in the 1900 Exhibition.

Plate 2 *Portrait of Rodenbach* by Lucien Lévy-Dhurmer. Pastel 1896. 14 × 22 in. (35 × 54 cm.). Musée Nationale d'Art Moderne, Paris.
Georges Rodenbach was one of the earliest Belgian Symbolist poets. Of Lévy-Dhurmer's portraits the critic Gabriel Mourey wrote: 'Here, as in all Lévy-Dhurmer does, we find the same striving to express the invisible and the deepseated, by means of that which is visible and on the surface. And this is evident not only in his constant endeavour to give character and style – if one may thus term it – to his model, but also in his habit of placing his subject in a setting corresponding to his own particular temperament, peculiarities and mode of life.'

Plate 3 *Sarah Bernhardt in the rôle of Ghismonda* by Walter Spindler. Oil on canvas. 1895. 66 × 42 in. (168 × 117 cm.). Emmerton-Lambert Collection.
Three women above all not only typified Art Nouveau in their persons but inspired as well the artists and designers of the period. Sarah Bernhardt, an androgynous figure so emaciated that in spite of being of average height she gave the impression of being enormously elongated, an effect she accentuated by wearing long waistless dresses of bizarre design and by reclining in carefully contrived curves, was a major source of inspiration not only to her protegé Alphonse Mucha but to other painters as well.

Loie Fuller, the American dancer (see next plate), was transformed by her veils and coloured lights into a vague shifting image which could be interpreted as a flower, a flame, a butterfly, a wisp of smoke. To the Symbolist poets she appeared as the embodiment of their dreams while to painters and sculptors the beauty of this ephemeral vision was a challenge to their powers of rendering the fleeting image in clay or on canvas.

The last member of this trio of muses was Cléo de Mérode (plate 14), a dancer with a classical training in the Paris Opera Ballet. Her appeal was simpler. She was, by popular vote, the most beautiful woman in France and time and time again one sees sculptured and painted nymphs with her perfect oval face and with her characteristic coiffure, the simplicity of which was all the more striking at a time when coiffures were extremely elaborate.

Plate 4 *Loie Fuller* by Marie-Félix Hippolyte Lucas. *c.* 1898. Oil on canvas. 35 × 45 in. (89 × 114 cm.). Private Collection, Brighton.

Painted soon after the American dancer's debut at the Folies-Bergère in 1893, this slightly idealized likeness shows 'The Divine Loie' rather more undraped than she appeared on the stage. Little is known of Lucas's work beyond the bare facts that he first exhibited at the Salon of 1877, and executed decorative murals at the Casino at Monte-Carlo and the 1900 Exhibition. This portrait suggests that he was considerably more accomplished than many of his contemporaries.

Loie Fuller's overnight success as a dancer after being for many years a moderately successful actress led to her being depicted by many painters and sculptors who endeavoured to convey the magic of her performances (see previous note). Her theatre, which formed one of the attractions of the 1900 Exhibition was designed for her by Henri Sauvage with sculptured decorations by Pierre Roche, was a small masterpiece of Art Nouveau design. In spite of her fame this country girl from Illinois retained a simplicity which gained her the lifelong friendship of Rodin, Marie Curie, and Anatôle France. Among her protegées were the celebrated Japanese actress Sada Yacco and the young Isadora Duncan whose ingratitude caused Loie Fuller great pain. Her school of dancing did not survive her death in 1928 at the age of 66.

Plate 5 *Robert de Montesquiou* by Giovanni Boldini. 1897. 44½ × 32½ in. (113 × 82 cm.). Musée Nationale d'Art Moderne, Paris.

The Symbolist poet Robert de Montesquiou commissioned most of the leading portrait painters of his day, including Whistler, to record his features for posterity; unfortunately for his hopes he is remembered for his eccentricities and not at all for his poems. His portrait by Giovanni Boldini brought together two of the most extraordinary personalities in Paris.

Montesquiou, tall, slender, an aristocrat and a dandy, the original of Proust's Baron de Charlus, was the patron of Emile Gallé and the protector of Verlaine in his last miseries. Boldini was one of a brood of children fathered by a starving Italian painter from whom he had learnt a tight meticulous technique. He had made his way to Paris where an acquaintance with the slashing technique of Anders Zorn changed his life.

Almost a dwarf he fascinated his sitters by his method of painting, gazing at them intently as though to draw out their inmost secrets and then attacking the canvas with long brushes held at arm's length. He transformed his sitters into almost impossibly seductive creatures striking languorous poses and suggesting that the slightest movement would result in the beautifully painted silks, chiffons, lace and chinchilla falling off to reveal them in writhing nudity. His male portraits show a deeper realisation of character and personality.

Plate 6 *Metal balustrade for a staircase* by Louis Majorelle. *c.* 1900. 33 × 83 in. (85 × 210 cm) Musée des Arts Decoratifs, Paris.

The Majorelle factory at Nancy had a section devoted to metalwork where lamps and the elaborate metal mounts which are a characteristic feature of Majorelle's furniture, were produced (see plate 12). There are also a number of gold flecked orange or mauve glass bowls and vases signed 'Daum' which appear to have been blown into a decorative metal framework, usually of hammered iron which bears the signature of Majorelle. The plant called 'Lunaire' or Honesty was utilised as basis for design by a number of artists at this period.

Plate 7 *Vitrine in fruitwood c.* 1898. 60 × 24 × 11 in. (153 × 61 × 28 cm.). Private Collection, Brighton.

This consists of a showcase with glazed door and sides lined with the original sage-green velvet and containing three adjustable glass shelves, an open compartment below and a narrow shelf on each side. It is in the manner of the simpler pieces produced by the Gallé workshops but the absence of any signature or other means of identification precludes a definite attribution. The stencilled mark of the firm at the back (Chartaux, Boulogne-sur-Mer) does not necessarily mean that it was made in Boulogne but may have been manufactured elsewhere – the firm acting as a selling agent. Such a piece of furniture was typical of the light graceful accessories of a boudoir or salon and is shown containing ornaments which were fashionable at the time. The mid-nineteenth century custom of covering every available surface with ornaments was still prevalent.

Top Shelf:

Gilt bronze vase by E. Maurel in the shape of a poppy-head decorated with a design of poppies in low relief and a naturalistic lizard in full relief. Height 5½ in. (14 cm.)

Vase for a single flower by Emil Gallé (plate 34)

Bronze bust by Godet (plate 19)

Middle Shelf:

Bronze electric lamp by Jozen (plate 19)

Glass vase by Emil Gallé (plate 34)

Porcelain vase with the glaze known as 'couverte à cristallisation grand feu de four', from Sèvres. Height 4½ in. (11 cm.)

Lower Shelf:

Greenish bronze figure of a dancing girl by Flamand, with a shell headdress and holding flowing draperies in her outstretched hands. Height 9 in. (23 cm.)

Open Compartment:

Gilt Bronze two handled flower bowl by Marchand. (plate 46)

Plates 8, 9 *Inlaid worktable of ash* by Emil Gallé. 1900. 30 × 27⅝ × 14¾ in. (76 × 70 × 38 cm.). Bethnal Green Museum, London.

Firescreen of ash by Emil Gallé. 1900. 42¼ × 21¾ × 14 in. (118 × 55 × 36 cm.). Bethnal Green Museum, London.

Emil Gallé was born in 1846 and became one of the greatest artists in glass of any period (see plates 33 and 34). In 1884 he turned his attention to the design of furniture, believing that the same decorative idiom, based on natural forms, should apply to all the furnishings of a house. At first the forms of his furniture were strongly influenced by the pastiches of Louis XV and Renaissance then in fashion, with the difference that they were decorated with flowers of inlaid veneers, landscapes and quotations from poets he admired – a feature already to be found in his glasswork. The worktable here has the inscription 'Work is joy at the house of Gallé' inlaid into the table surface. His finer pieces, those executed under his close personal supervision, were intended to be embodiments of ideas or solid realisation of Symbolist poems as can be seen from their names, for example a cabinet or a salon entitled 'Perfumes of other days' and vases with such names as 'The Snows of Pentecost'. As Gallé had a large factory to maintain a great amount of purely commercial furniture and glass had to be produced with a lowering of quality and although each of these pieces bore Gallé's signature they are less interesting than the individually created works such as the 'Hortensia commode' commissioned by Robert de Montesquiou and exhibited in Paris and London in 1892.

Gallé's influence on the decorative arts was considerable. He was the centre of a coterie of designers, Victor Prouvé, the Daum brothers, Louis Majorelle and others based in Nancy but regularly exhibiting in Paris – Gallé's glass and furniture could be bought at A La Paix in the Avenue de l'Opéra.

Plate 10 *Cabinet for a music-room in sycamore* by Alexandre Charpentier. 1900. 79 × 92 × 25½ in. (200 × 234 × 64 cm.) Musée des Arts Décoratifs, Paris.

The centre compartment has two glazed doors and was intended to store musical instruments, music being kept in the side compartments. This cabinet with two music stands en suite was exhibited at the Salon of 1901. The two shaped panels contain gilt bronze reliefs, on the left 'L'Alto' on the right 'La Contrebasse'. The other panels represent dancers and are in Charpentier's distinctive technique. The flowing lines like the stems of flowers contrasted with the emphatic verticals of the glazed doors give the cabinet a superficial resemblance to Hector Guimard's iron entrances to the Métro (figure 4). Criticisms were made that the design of the curved supports of the cabinet and more particularly the supports of the music stands was more suitable to metal than to wood, a material subject to distortion through differences of temperature and atmosphere. Sycamore was the favourite wood of a number of designers at this period.

Alexandre Charpentier (1856-1909) had gained fame through his execution of portrait medallions. Convinced that good design should be applied to all objects whether decorative or useful, he turned his attention to furniture which he adorned with bas-reliefs or three dimensional sculpture. He was one of the original members of 'Les Cinq' together with Charles Plumet, the architect, Jean Dampt, the sculptor, Moreau-Nélaton, the painter and critic and Félix Aubert whose speciality was the designing of textiles and wall-papers. In 1898 the group became 'Les Six' by the addition of Pierre Selmersheim who continued to collaborate with Plumet on architectural schemes for some years after the disbanding of the original nucleus. This short-lived association of different talents was formed with the intention of exhibiting to the public original and useful objects which had received the same care and attention as works of art.

Plate 11 *Inlaid tray* by Louis Majorelle, fitted with brass handles. 1900. 25½ × 16⅛ in. (65 × 42 cm.) Bethnal Green Museum, London.

The designs for marquetry on furniture by Majorelle and Gallé were often done by Victor Prouvé (1858-1943), a friend from childhood of the latter. A close collaborator of Gallé and to a lesser extent of Majorelle, Victor Prouvé spent most of his life in Paris working as a sculptor and bookbinder and was a valuable link between the creative life in Paris and Nancy.

Plate 12 *Inlaid cabinet* by Majorelle. 1900. 71¾ × 26¾ × 18¼ in. (183 × 67 × 47 cm.). Bethnal Green Museum, London.

The Vice-President of the jury for awards in the 1900 Paris Exhibition, Sir George Donaldson, wanted to familiarise English designers and manufacturers with the 'New Art' in Europe. Realizing that no public funds were available, he very generously decided to present a number of pieces of furniture, pottery and metalwork for exhibition to the South Kensington Museum, amongst them the Gallé worktable and firescreen (plates 8 and 9) and this cabinet, which combines patterns of veneers with metal embellishments. Unfortunately the exhibits excited such criticism from various institutions connected with the arts that they were quickly withdrawn from public exhibition.

Plate 13 *Tall clock* by Hector Guimard. *c.* 1898. 94½ × 15 in. (240 × 38 cm.). Musée des Arts Décoratifs, Paris.

Hector Guimard's most famous creation was his scheme for the entrances to the Paris Métro and it is for these that he is mainly remembered. Much of his work in interior decoration and furniture has been lost to sight, but enough remains to indicate that he was one of the major talents in the Art Nouveau movement.

Plate 14 *Occasional table* of tripod form with shaped undershelf, inlaid in various woods with designs of lilac and butterflies, by Louis Majorelle. Height 30 in. (66 cm.). Private Collection, Brighton.

Chair in rosewood with semi-cabriole legs and a carved open-work back, by Eugène Colonna. Private Collection, Brighton.

The original of this chair – in satinwood – was designed by Colonna as part of the furnishings of the salon of Bing's exhibit 'La Maison de l'Art Nouveau' at the 1900 Paris Universal Exhibition and was reproduced in *The Studio* volume 20. Gabriel Mourey, the *Studio* correspondent in Paris was not an ardent admirer of the Art Nouveau style but for once he waxed lyrical over Colonna's salon and indeed over the design and decoration of Bing's pavilion as a whole. Although Bing's patronage did not extend to such great names as Gallé, Daum, Majorelle or Lalique, 'La Maison de l'Art Nouveau' with its rooms designed by Lucien Gaillard, Georges de Feure, and Eugène Colonna was probably the culminating point of Art Nouveau, demonstrating the application of the style to every room – except a kitchen – and achieving at the same time an effect of luxurious elegance.

Ashtray in gilt bronze of irregular shape, decorated with the head and arms of a baby in relief, by Betlen. 1900. Private Collection.

The incised letters 'MM' on the base indicate that it came from La Maison Moderne and two pieces of sculpture by Betlen are illustrated in the firm's catalogue issued in 1901 under the title of *Documents sur l'Art Industriel au XXe Siècle*. Unfortunately the firm's aim (to bring examples of the avant-garde movement within the financial reach of most people) resulted in a lowering of standards of design which undoubtedly led to its early failure.

Glass flower vase cut with a design of irises, by Baccarat. c. 1898. Height 10¼ in. (27 cm.) Private Collection.

Le Livre d'Or issued to commemorate the gala in honour of Sarah Bernhardt given at the Théâtre de la Renaissance on December 9th 1896.

A glittering gathering drawn from society and the arts applauded Madame Bernhardt as she performed extracts from her greatest successes prior to her being enthroned and crowned with a wreath of laurels while a number of poets recited their odes in her praise. The occasion was announced by a poster by Alphonse Mucha while *Le Livre d'Or* with an embossed gold cover by Alexandre Charpentier contained a programme of the day's events, poems illustrated by the celebrated artistic friends of the actress, Louise Abbéma (plate 16), Clairin, Carolus Duran, and Lalique whose profile gold medal of the Divine Sarah was reproduced.

Cléo de Mérode. Photograph by Reutlinger.

One of the best selling photographs of the dancer, voted the most beautiful woman in France in 1896 shortly after she had adopted the severe hairstyle which became identified with her. This was reproduced on thousands of postcards subsequently.

Les Hortensias Bleus. Poems by Robert de Montesquiou-Fesenzac. 1906.

The definitive edition with a frontispiece of the portrait of the poet by de Laszlo and a prefatory poem written in memory of his friend Gabriel de Yturri who had died the previous year and beside whom Montesquiou was buried in 1921.

Plate 15 *Dressing table in sycamore* with gilt bronze handles. The shaped mirror flanked by two small circular shelves for lamps. The table has a sunk plate glass top and five drawers, one of which is divided into compartments for toilet accessories. Overall height 55 in, width 42 in., depth 29 in. (140 × 106 × 74 cm.). Private Collection.

The use of light coloured wood, the moiré-like veneeer on the flat surfaces and, in particular, the design of the handles on this piece of furniture would indicate its having been designed by Georges de Feure; however the use of a curved strut rising out of the leg to form an upright between the centre and side drawers is characteristic of the work of Abel Landry, designer of the greater part of the furniture for La Maison Moderne.

Metal electric lamp. The base of entwined scrolls and flowers; a helmeted female figure poised on a ball and supporting scrolls which terminate in nautilus shells concealing electric light bulbs. Height 25 in. (65 cm.) Private Collection.

Typical of a number of similar lamps combining silvered metal and real shells which appear to have been produced in different versions using castings in various combinations. Real mother-of-pearl had been used at an earlier period for candleshades but the invention of small electric light bulbs enabled designers to conceal the source of light within the shell. Nautilus shells were used a few years later by Paul Poiret in the decorative schemes produced by his firm L'Atelier Martine for applied to the ceiling they solved the problem of concealing a centre light, giving a suffused light without glare.

Gilt bronze ashtray by Marchand, composed of scrolls surrounding a female head, with flowing hair, a spray of mistletoe forming a handle. Length 7½ in. (19 cm.)

Gilded metal jug with handle by Charles Perron. Height 8¼ in. (21 cm.)
Inspired by an eighteenth-century original the body of the jug is decorated in low relief with nymphs swimming in water which gushes from the mask of a bearded man; a three dimensional figure of a nude nymph climbs up to look into the interior of the vessel.

Bronze paperweight by Muller. Portrait bust of Cléo de Mérode emerging from sprays of mistletoe and wearing a bandeau decorated with mistletoe berries. Height 7 in. (18 cm.)

Gilt bronze paperknife by M. Bouval. The blade in the shape of a leaf, the handle composed of a nude female figure wreathed with smaller leaves. Length 9 in. (23 cm.)

Novels in France were sold at this period with the pages uncut, so paperknives were a necessity and many designs can be found which use the favourite motifs of Art Nouveau – women and flowers – in endless variations.

Le chef des odeurs suaves. Poems by Robert de Montesquiou. Copy presented to the painter Walter Spindler by the author on June 3rd 1894 and inscribed 'Affectueuse Souvenir du "Jardinièr des jacinthes de l'Isräel"'. One of two hundred copies printed for the author and bound in olive green morocco with designs of cyclamen inlaid in blue and violet leather. The name of the volume is taken from a character in Gustave Flaubert's *Salammbo* and contains poems dedicated to Paul Helleu, Emil Gallé, Whistler and the poet's cousin, la Comtesse Greffuhle.

Plate 16 *Portrait of a lady with chrysanthemums* by Louise Abbéma. Oil on canvas. (1858-1927). 47 × 35 in. (120 × 91 cm.). Private Collection, Brighton.
A similar painting of a head and shoulders enclosed in an oval architectural opening decorated with roses can be seen in a photograph of Louise Abbéma in her studio reproduced in *Femina* for May 1903. The portrait illustrated was probably intended as a companion painting. A tiny woman, Louise Abbéma combined a noticeably masculine appearance with a feminine talent, specialised in portraits of society beauties and was said to be 'one of the first to understand the beauty of that silent poem we call a flower'. She was the pupil of two indifferent painters – Chaplin and Henner – and one good one, Carolus-Duran, and came to the notice of the public by her entry for the Salon of 1876, a portrait of Sarah Bernhardt whose devoted admirer she remained for the rest of her life. Her decorative murals in the Hôtel

de Ville de Paris, the town halls of several arrondisements of Paris and the Governor's Palace at Dakar earned her many official awards culminating in her being made a Chevalier of the Légion d'Honneur in 1906.

Portrait bust in gilt bronze by Raoul Larche. Height 18½ in. (47 cm.) Private Collection, Brighton.

Réve Fleuri and *Reveil Printanier*. Figures of nymphs entwined with overscaled flowers, the centres of which incorporate electric light bulbs. Tinted composition. Height 43 in. (110 cm.) Private Collection, Brighton.

These figures are similar to and may have been inspired by the life-size bronze figures 'Le Reveil' and 'Le Sommeil' by Joseph Chéret (the brother of Jules Chéret, the poster designer) which stood until its demolition in the foyer of that movie-palace to end all movie-palaces, the Roxy in New York. Chéret's gambolling cupids have been replaced by giant flowers of the poppy family but the nymphs have the same absentminded abandon. Electricity was still a comparative novelty and no attempt was made to conceal the bulbs which gave a much softer light than their modern counterparts. These figures were probably intended for a café or restaurant where Art Nouveau was given a freer rein than elsewhere.

Plate 17 *Pair of electric lamps of metal* by L. Allion with a greenish finish modelled as draped female figures holding yoke-like scrolls which support the light sockets. The dresses of the figures end in openwork decorative scrolls which form a base for the figures. Height 16½ in. (42 cm.). Private Collection.

Bronzed metal electric lamp by L. Allion in the form of a dancing figure in a flowing robe, the light bulb concealed in the drapery held over the head of the figure. Height 17 in. (43 cm.). Private Collection.

Gilt bronze ashtray with figure whose draperies form the tray by Rubin. Height 3½ in. (9 cm.). Private Collection.

Plate 18 *Bronze wall plaque* by Léchu of a nymph in low relief reclining on a crescent moon amid clouds and grasping a star; other stars and two small *putti* appear in the background. Inscribed with the founder's name 'Susse Frères Paris'. 14½ × 20 in. (37 × 51 cm.). Private Collection, Brighton.

Bronze shell-shaped dish by J. Garnier of a siren in low relief reposing on a wave holding an archaic harp and watching the sails of a ship in the distance. 6¼ × 10 in. (16 × 25 cm.). Private Collection.

Iron shell-shaped dish by J. Garnier of a sleeping nymph resting on the surface of the sea. 7½ × 12 in. (19 × 30 cm.). Private Collection.

Decorative wall plaques of this type were exported from France in considerable numbers, under the name of 'Articles de Paris'. Susse Frères, Barbadienne and other firms would buy the copyright of reliefs and other pieces of decorative sculpture from the artists. They would then reproduce them in various forms for sale at home and abroad.

Plate 19 *Greenish bronze dish* in the shape of a water-lily leaf terminating in a portrait head of Cléo de Mérode, by Angles. Length 8 in. (20 cm.). Private Collection.

Bronze bust of a girl emerging from a flower with green onyx base, by Godet. Height 8½ in. (21½ cm.). Private Collection.

Bronze electric lamp by Jozen. The light fitting is concealed in the centre of an iris which rises from a water-lily leaf upon which is seated a pensive nude nymph. Inscribed 'Salon des Beaux Arts'. Height 9 in. (23 cm.). Private Collection.

Robert de Montesquiou, in his poem *Blumenmädchen* summed up the absorption of so many of the designers of the Art Nouveau period with women and flowers in association in the line 'Fleur-femme, femme-fleur, laquelle est le plus l'autre?' and continues the theme with references to Wagner's flower-maidens in *Parsifal*, the 'Fleurs Animées' of Grandville, the flower-strewn robes of Botticelli's nymphs and the drawings of Walter Crane, whose acquaintance he had made when he came to London to sit for portraits by Whistler. Appreciation of the beauties of the female nude were combined with an equally sensuous delight in flowers, new varieties of which were arriving from Japan. Edmond de Goncourt was sent forty rare paeonies from the Far East by the dealer Hayashi in 1888 and was entranced by the poetry of the Japanese names for the different varieties. A common interest in horticulture led Montesquiou to become the patron of Emil Gallé who created furniture, as well as glass for him.

Plate 20 *Gilt bronze inkwell*, by Raoul Larche, depicting a nymph sitting on rocks, clasping a spray of oak-leaves and acorns; a drapery conceals her left leg and continues to form part of the base. A section of the rocks is hinged and lifts to disclose a glass inkwell. 19 × 23 in. (48 × 59 cm.)
François Raoul Larche was one of the sculptors employed on a free-lance basis by the Sèvres Manufactory. Like most of the sculptors of the latter part of the nineteenth century, most of whom have suffered from the subsequent eclipse of their reputations by Rodin, he depended less upon commissions than upon the royalties to be obtained from the mass production of small pieces of sculpture. The inkwell illustrated is of unusually imposing dimensions and would have been intended as an exhibition piece or for an embassy where its size would have been appropriate.

Plate 21 *Gilt bronze wall clock* with semi-draped figures of 'Day' and 'Night' surrounding the dial. Cast by Daubrée from a model by Moreau-Vauthier. Height 8 in. (20 cm.). Private Collection.
Gabriel Jean Paul Moreau-Vauthier was the creator of the most controversial statue in the 1900 Exhibition, that sur-

mounting the monumental entrance in the Place Concorde (see frontispiece).

Plate 22 *La Cothurne*. Gilt bronze figure of a dancer in 'Greek' robes adjusting her shoe, after a model by Agathon Léonard. Height 10¾ in. (27 cm.). Foundry mark of Susse Frères. Private Collection.
Loie Fuller. Gilt bronze figure with an electric light fitting concealed in the billowing drapery, after a model by Raoul Larche. Height 12½ in. (31½ cm.). Foundry mark of Susse Frères. Private Collection.
Dancer. Gilt bronze figure, after a model by Agathon Léonard. Height 12 in. (30 cm.). Foundry mark of Susse Frères. Private Collection.
Originally modelled in white biscuit porcelain these two Greek dancers are from a set of eight created by Agathon Léonard, intended as decorations for a dining table. They were immediately successful when they were exhibited in the Sèvres pavilion at the 1900 Exhibition. Individual figures could be ordered and 'La Cothurne' proved the most popular. A later and coarser version was produced in several sizes, the pleated dresses simplified and with decoration resembling broderie-anglaise round the sleeves and hems. Their success led to the firm of Susse buying the right to cast versions in metal – of which these are examples – and in some cases the pose and draperies were altered to incorporate a small electric light as in the second figure where a bulb is concealed in the floating scarf. Raoul Larche's sculpture of Loie Fuller was one of several attempts to reproduce the wraith-like appearance of the dancer.

Plate 23 *Ice Fairy*. Draped figure of a girl by J. Caussé with flowers in her hair in silvered metal with oxydised finish standing on a base of opalescent glass representing melting ice, by Leveillée of Nancy. Height 23½ in. (60 cm.)

This must have been made prior to 1900 when it was illustrated in *L'Art Décoratif*. Caussé, a pupil of Falguière, was one of the many sculptors producing the 'bronzes d'art' which were so much in demand at this period.

Plate 24 *Silver group* of a water nymph pursued by a triton, the shaped base of verde antique marble on silver feet, by Léo Laporte-Blairsy. 18½ × 24 in. (47 × 61 cm.). Private Collection.

Léo Laporte-Blairsy, who sometimes signed his work 'Léo Laporte' was a designer of jewellery and silver ornaments. He had a liking for marine motifs and some of his work was illustrated in *L'Art Décoratif* for 1903.

Plates 25, 26 *Door Furniture* by Alexandre Charpentier. *c.* 1896. Fingerplates 2¾ × 19 in. (7 × 48 cm.). Doorknobs *c.* 3 × 2 in. (8 × 5 cm.). Plaques for locks 3¼ × 5¾ in. (8 × 15 cm.). Victoria and Albert Museum, London.

When the interest in medals, hitherto neglected, was revived during this period Alexandre Charpentier found immediate favour with his naturalistic technique and his nude, unromanticised figures which seem to be emerging from the surface of the metal. The originality of his talent was soon realised and his portrait medallions of such celebrities as Edmond de Goncourt were much in demand among collectors. The door furniture illustrated was commissioned from him by the firm of Fontaine.

Plate 27 *Pottery vase* by Edmond Lachenal. *c.* 1893. Height 12½ in. (32 cm.). Private Collection.

Edmond Lachenal was esteemed by his contemporaries as one of the foremost ceramic artists of the day and his work was greatly influenced by Japanese Art as can be seen in the decoration of this important vase with its device of bamboo in relief, the indigo glaze of the stems and leaves contrast-

ing with the brilliant turquoise ground. Several versions of this design were made in porcelain as well as pottery, some with thick incrustations of white glaze to represent snow. In addition to vases with elaborate floral decorations Lachenal created vases of simple shapes which showed to advantage the beauty of the *Email Velouté* which he invented – the effect of a velvety finish to the glaze which was obtained by giving the finished vessel a bath of acid. Lachenal was a pupil of Théodore Deck the pioneer of the revival of interest in reproducing the coloured glazes and decorations of Rhodian, Persian and, at a later date, Chinese pottery. In 1880, at the age of 25, Lachenal founded his own pottery at Chatillon-sous-Baigneux and in the 1890s he held several exhibitions, collaborated with Rodin, and turned less successfully to furniture design.

Plate 28 *Porcelain vase* in eggshell blue with silver mount and handles, possibly by Dufrène. *c.* 1895. 7⅜ × 4⅞ in. (19 × 12 cm.). Victoria and Albert Museum, London.

Two earthenware vases with bronzed lustre finish, by Clément Massier. 6¾ × 2⅝ in. (17 × 7 cm.). 6¼ × 4⅜ in. (16 × 11 cm.). Victoria and Albert Museum, London.

Clément Massier perfected this iridescent glaze which was inspired by what he had seen on Hispano-Moresque pots. The pattern may have been suggested by Lévy-Dhurmer the painter, who collaborated with Clément-Massier for a while.

Plate 29 *Iridescent plaque* by Clément Massier. *c.* 1898. 15 in. (38 cm.). Collection Luigi Visconti, Ischia.

The well-known Art Nouveau theme of a naked woman with flowing draperies is used again here and the iridescence enhances the effect of movement and mystery.

Plate 30 *Four pieces of pottery* by E. Decoeur. *c.* 1901. Heights from 4½ – 11½ in. (11½ – 29 cm.). Bethnal Green Museum.

These are in heavy porcelain with brown, cream and grey crackle glaze, one with a pattern of scrolls. They are reminiscent of Chinese pottery in their simple shapes and subtle glazing.

Small decorative plaque by Taxile Doat. 1901. 1½ × 3¾ in. (4 × 5½ cm.). Bethnal Green Museum, London.

This was probably intended for part of a decorative scheme (with 'La Terre' and so on) although it might also have been used as a paperweight. It is made of hard porcelain ornamented with paste decoration and enhanced by coloured glazes of different textures.

Plate 31 *Porcelain vase* with pale green glaze, by Auguste Rodin. 9¾ in. (25 cm.). Private Collection.

Rodin was employed by the Sèvres Factory in the early 80s, after his struggles for recognition had been fruitless and his statue 'L'Age d'Airan' had aroused hostility in 1877 when it was first shown. The individuality and power of his creations had aroused the antagonism of the academic school, no commissions were available and the comparatively menial tasks he had to perform at the Sèvres Factory enabled him to live. His vigorous energy was hampered by the need for delicate detail and the results do not show him at his fullest capacity. Carrier-Belleuse, whose sculptures can be found adorning the Paris Opera House, had a short association with the Sèvres factory in 1882.

Plate 32 *Porcelain vase with gilt bronze mounts.* Decorated with painting in tones of pink, mushroom and celadon green. Inscribed 'Décoré à Sèvres, 1905'. Height 9½ in. (24 cm.). Private Collection.

The conventionalised floral decoration shows the transition from naturalism to the geometrical renderings of 'Art Déco' the style which superseded Art Nouveau in the latter years of the first decade of the twentieth century and culminated in the 1925 Exhibition.

Plate 33 *Bottle of straw-coloured glass* with enamel decoration of a dragonfly, a butterfly and conventionalised flowers in tones of pink, white and blue, by Emil Gallé. *c.* 1889. 5½ in. (14 cm.). Private Collection.

Dark green vase with ribbed and flared base with design in relief of orchids and fungi etched inside and out, by Emil Gallé. *c.* 1895. 14 in. (35½ cm.). Private Collection.

Dark pink vase cased in reddish-brown glass etched in designs of trees and bare branches by the Daum brothers. *c.* 1895. 11¼ in. (28½ cm.). Private Collection.

Emil Gallé's creations owe much to Oriental examples of glassware and yet his work is an expression of his personal interests and temperament. He is certainly one of the chief originators of the Art Nouveau movement since he was producing glass like this in the mid-80s. The Daum brothers, Auguste and Antonin, are indebted to him although their finely-conceived pieces are notable in their own right.

Plate 34 *Red and yellow vase* with ring handles by Emil Gallé, etched and enamelled with designs of flowers in various colours and incorporating gold leaf. *c.* 1889. 9½ in. (24 cm.). Private Collection.

Pale pink flower vase with globular shape and tall neck by Emil Gallé, overlaid with orange glass cut away in a design of nasturtiums. *c.* 1893. 4 in. (10 cm.). Private Collection.

White vase shading to pink by Emil Gallé, with dark purple overlay cut away in a flower design. *c.* 1893. 6 in. (15 cm.). Private Collection.

Trumpet-shaped vase with white and violet ground cut with field flowers picked out in enamel, by the Daum brothers. *c.* 1895. 11½ in. (29 cm.). Private Collection.

Plate 35 *Glass inkwell* by the Daum brothers, the lid formed of a conventionalised anemone with yellowish cream opaque glass, the base engraved with foliage. Private Collection.

Plate 36 *Pâte-de-verre vase* by G. Argy-Rousseau. Opaque off-white ground with faint streaks of colour; two decorative motifs in relief of a red faun mask with wreaths of ivy in purple and green. Height 4 in. (10 cm.). Private Collection. *Pâte-de-verre dish*, the streaked blue and green ground decorated with three clusters of berries and leaves in red and green. Diameter 6 in. (15 cm.). Private Collection.

Bowl of pâte-de-verre by G. Argy-Rousseau, decorated with asymmetrical sprays of berries and leaves in red and olive green. Height 2⅝ in. (7 cm.). Private Collection.

Pâte-de-verre (glass paste) is the name given to the process by which powdered glass of different colours is packed into a mould and then fired, the heat fusing the powder into a solid mass with a resemblance to tinted alabaster. The sculptor Henry Cros who worked for the Sèvres Factory is credited with perfecting this technique by means of which he hoped to recreate the effect of polychrome sculpture, combining form and colour in one creative effort. The success of these efforts led to his process being used by other glass workers such as Daum and possibly Gallé, although it is not always easy to distinguish between true pâte-de-verre and ordinary glass which has been treated with acid to give a rough finish. A younger generation of individual glass workers, Argy-Rousseau, Dammouse and Decorchement made numerous vases and small plaques in pâte-de-verre until the mid 1920s when the use of this technique became unfashionable. After 1900 the firms of Walter, Schneider and Muller mass-produced pâte-de-verre lampshades which were combined with wrought iron frameworks in the manner of Edgar Brandt.

Plate 37 *Brooch* by Marcel Bing. *c.* 1900. 2 × 1½ in. (5 × 4 cm.). Musée des Arts Décoratifs, Paris.
This is in gilded copper, enamel and a garnet, featuring a woman with flowing hair, a headdress of medieval inspiration from which depend wings in blue and green cloisonné enamel. A version of this brooch, identical in design but with the face and neck of the woman carved in ivory, was exhibited at L'Art Nouveau in 1900.

Plate 38 *Six enamel buttons* decorated with heads of women symbolising various flowers and fruit, which are named on the back of each button in gold letters, 'Pomme', 'Groseille', 'Yris', 'Capucine', 'Cerises', 'Orangers'. Private Collection. *Silver pillbox* decorated with white translucent enamel on an engine turned ground. The lid bears the head of a woman, her hair entwined with poppies, executed in multicoloured enamels. Diameter 2 in. (5 cm.). English import mark for 1901. Private Collection.

This design shows an obvious affinity with the work of Alphonse Mucha.

Plate 39 *Silver gilt buckle* with a design of irises by René Lalique. 1897. 3½ × 2½ in. (9 × 6 cm.). Victoria and Albert Museum, London.
This was illustrated in *Art et Décoration* 1897. For further details on Lalique, see Introduction page 7.

Plate 40 *Hair ornament and buckle* en suite by René Lalique made of horn and gilded metal, with topaz and carved glass inset. *c.* 1900. 6½ × 1¾ in. (16½ × 4½ cm.). 5⅛ × 1¾ in. (13 × 4½ cm.). Victoria and Albert Museum, London.

Plate 41 *Silver lorgnette* by Camille Gueyton. *c.* 1900. Length 8½ in. (21½ cm.). Private Collection.
The silversmith Camille Gueyton combined symmetrical outlines with naturalistic floral decorations in relief asymetrically arranged as in a dish illustrated in *La Grande Dame* for 1894 where he uses palm fronds as a motif. He was particularly fond of showing the front of a marguerite with a

gold centre on one side of an object, the back of the blossom appearing on the reverse side.

Silver cigarette case embossed with design of mistletoe. *c.* 1900. 2½ × 3½ in. (6 × 9 cm.). Private Collection, Brighton.
The mistletoe device is typical of the taste for strange and slightly ambiguous motifs (mistletoe is not unlike an insect).

Silver plaquette by Henri Kautsch. 1905. Height 2¾ in. (7 cm.). Private Collection.
The original model for this medallion was exhibited at the Société Nationale des Beaux-Arts and was illustrated in Volume 35 of *The Studio*. Medallions of this kind were intended to be used as awards, the reverse having a simple design of a laurel wreath and a panel where the name of the recipient could be inscribed. In this case the award was to an English student at the University of Grenoble.

Bronze medal by Henri Dubois. *c.* 1900. Height 2⅜ in. (6 cm.). Private Collection.
This medal bears a close resemblance to one by Alexandre Charpentier illustrated in *The Studio* for 1902. The reverse is similar to that of the Kautsch medal.

Plate 42 *Lorgnette* by René Lalique. Shaped like a lizard and made of gold, enamel and precious stones. 6½ in. (16 cm.). Musée des Arts Décoratifs, Paris.

Plate 43 *Miscellaneous Jewellery. c.* 1900. Private Collections. This is typical of the more conventional kind of jewellery which was produced in considerable quantity especially after the 1900 Exhibition. In the autumn of that year similar jewellery was advertised in English magazines.

Plate 44 *Six silver spoons* in the shape of flowers and stems, a letter opener and a bookmark with floral decorations by Prince Bogdar Karageorgevitch. Lengths from 4¾ – 7⅜ in. (12 – 19 cm.). Victoria and Albert Museum, London.

Prince Karageorgevitch was one of the artists whose work could be found at La Maison Moderne about 1901. He was also a journalist and writer of art and an article by him on Gallé was in *The Magazine of Art* for 1904.

Plate 45 *Documents Décoratifs* by Alphonse Mucha. Plate 29. Published by Librairie Centrale des Beaux-Arts. 1902. Private Collection.
A portfolio of 72 loose plates of reproductions of designs by Mucha issued in 1902 with an introduction by Gabriel Mourey (the Paris correspondent of *The Studio*). The collection was a miscellany of designs for jewellery, furniture, lace, and so on, interspersed with botanical studies, figure drawings and versions of the posters and decorative panels which had made Mucha's work so popular. A companion volume *Figures Décoratives* (1908) was devoted entirely to studies of nude and draped female figures, some of which show Mucha abandoning the Art Nouveau motifs of women combined with flowers in favour of the costume and national characteristics of his native country.

Cloches de Noël et de Pâques by Emile Gebhart. Illustrations and decorations by A. Mucha. No. 141 of an edition limited to 252 copies. Published 1900. Private Collection.
Three short stories *Les Trois Rois, La Dernière Nuit de Jésus* and *Alleluia!* Each page has the text enclosed in elaborate delicately coloured borders of conventionalised flowers of which there are thirty variations. The loose plates of the original have been rebound at a later date.

Paper Knife. Handle of silvered copper with stylised floral decoration. Blade of ivory. 13½ in. (34½ cm.). Private Collection.

Silver gilt cup with a conventional design of poppies by Fouquet. 2. in. (5 cm.). *c.* 1904. Private Collection.
The decoration of transparent coloured enamels on a tooled silver ground is adapted from Plate 29 of *Documents Déco-*

ratifs. Fouquet and Mucha worked in collaboration for many years.

Plate 46 *Bières de la Meuse*. Poster by Alphonse Mucha. Unfinished trial proof, signed 'Mucha' in two places. Lithograph on paper mounted on linen. 57 × 37½ in. (142 × 95 cm.). Private Collection.

Alphonse Mucha's output of designs for posters was considerably smaller than that of the indefatigable Jules Chéret but his work appeared on the streets of Paris at a time when the latter's agitated figures had become over-familiar and the novelty of Mucha's more static style and muted colours was in striking contrast. *Bières de la Meuse* is a comparatively late example of a poster by Mucha when his colour had tended to coarsen but this trial proof in black and white shows his masterful draughtsmanship and his characteristic treatment of drapery and hair. The uninspired views of the breweries in the lower panels may be by another hand.

Lamp and shade by Emile Gallé. Ground of yellow opaque glass, the superimposed layer of a deep amber colour being cut away in a design of asymmetrical sprays of flowers. Signed 'Gallé' on the base and on the shade. *c.* 1895. Height 28 in. (71 cm.). Width of shade 12 in. (30½ cm.). Private Collection.

A fine example of Gallé's more commercial products. The flowers have not been identified for in spite of Gallé's repute as a botanist, he frequently seems to have combined the blossoms of one plant with the leaves of another. The rapid growth of the use of electricity in lighting created new forms of lampshades – this enclosed example could not have been used on an oil-lamp. There is provision made in the metal fitting which supports the shade for a smaller bulb inside the glass base.

Gilt bronze flower container with panels of lilies-of-the-valley in relief by Debon. Width 12½ in. (32 cm.). Private Collection.

The French tradition of fine workmanship in gilt bronze or ormulu which had created so many magnificent objects from the seventeenth century onwards continued for a final manifestation during the last decade of the nineteenth century before disappearing in the twentieth century – apart from versions of antique models. This jardinière with its hand finished panels of naturalistic flowers bears the foundry mark of Susse Frères whose work was always of a fine quality.

Plate 47 *Loie Fuller*. Poster by Manuel Orazi. 1900. Private Collection.

A striking representation of the American dancer with her red hair as a focal point in the design. A very marked Japanese influence can be seen in this poster, the elongated shape being similar to that of a kakemono (a long narrow painting on silk hung vertically which was kept rolled when not on display) and the use of conventionalised Japanese family emblems which were used in the decoration of lacquer objects, brocades and the uniforms of the retainers of the family. This intensely Japanese influence reflects Loie Fuller's interest in the drama of that country and may have been a piece of indirect publicity for Sada Yacco a Japanese actress whom Miss Fuller, an impressario as well as a dancer, presented at her theatre in the 1900 Exhibition. Orazi contributed drawings and illustrations to periodicals and designed some jewellery for La Maison Moderne about 1900.

Plate 48 *Decorative panel* by Edouard Bénédictus. Colour lithograph from *Le Document du Décorateur* published by the Librairie d'Art Décoratif. *c.* 1900. Private Collection.

A collection of 48 lithographic reproductions of decorative paintings, fabrics, wallpapers, leatherwork, stained glass and ceramics by various artists and intended to be copied or interpreted by designers. These portfolios were produced in large numbers in France from the 1890s to the 1930s, the plates being at first reproduced in colour lithography and later by the 'Pochoir' process by means of which they were more accurately coloured by a silk screen process. Some collections were devoted to the work of a single artist, (plate 45) and the young Bénédictus whose work is represented in *Le Document du Décorateur* by five plates was later to have no less than three volumes of his designs, lavishly printed in many colours with the addition of gold and silver, published in the late 1920s. Originally a bookbinder Bénédictus changed his style as fashion demanded from Art Nouveau to the Art Décoratif of the twenties.

Plates 49 - 52 *Four reproductions of drawings* by Georges de Feure. Topogravures by Goupil. 1900. Private Collection. In the issue of February 1900 *Figaro Illustré* produced the second of a series of articles devoted to the subject of 'La Femme', written in this instance by Henri Frantz and illustrated with reproductions of drawings by Georges de Feure Like so many of his contemporaries de Feure was extremely versatile designing furniture, textiles and ceramics in addition to illustrating books and painting murals, all his work being characterised by subtlety of colour combined with elegance of form. Partly of Javanese origin he was more influenced by the art of Java than that of Japan. For years he collaborated with Samuel Bing designing furniture and textiles for the latter's gallery in the Rue de Provence. Bing's pavilion at the 1900 Exhibition was decorated outside with large painted panels by Georges de Feure and some rooms in the interior contained furniture, porcelain and textiles executed from his designs. He was possibly the only furniture designer of the period to use gilding in the traditional manner although he followed the current fashion favouring ve-

neers of pale coloured woods. His textiles with their gracefully conventionalised flowers were, like his porcelains, conceived in pale clear colours contrasted with areas of shades of grey and were in harmony with the furniture detailing.

From a modern viewpoint it is surprising to find that Henri Frantz, writing about de Feure's drawings found his charming decorative ladies sinister and redolent of evil and that he could class him among the artists who 'have opened the gates of Hell and revealed its nightmares... who have recorded forbidden sins...'.

Plates 53, 54 *Fleurs animées* 'Le Bluet' and 'L'Oillet'. Two decorative designs by Firmin Bouisset, reproduced in colour in *Figaro Illustré* for 1901. 12¾ × 6 in. (32 × 15 cm.). Private Collection.
Firmin Bouisset, the lithographer, was credited with having had a decisive influence upon the work of Alphonse Mucha. He specialised in depicting children drawn naturalistically and surrounded with elaborate scrolls of formalised leaves and flowers. He captured the changing moods of children without sentimentality and, modest in his ambitions, he was successful in his treatment of subject-matter not particularly popular with his contemporaries except Alexandre Charpentier. In addition to Bouisset's contributions to magazines he illustrated books for and about children, *Faits et Gestes d'Enfants* by the Abbé Briault (1890), *Les Memoires d'un Gros Sou* by Sylvia Consul, *La Petite Princesse* by Jeanne Mairet and for *Les Contes de Perrault*. His first poster was for Chocolat Meunier in 1892 followed by numerous others in the following years. His work, charming and gentle, was overshadowed by the bolder talents of Mucha and his many posters have almost been forgotten.

2

4

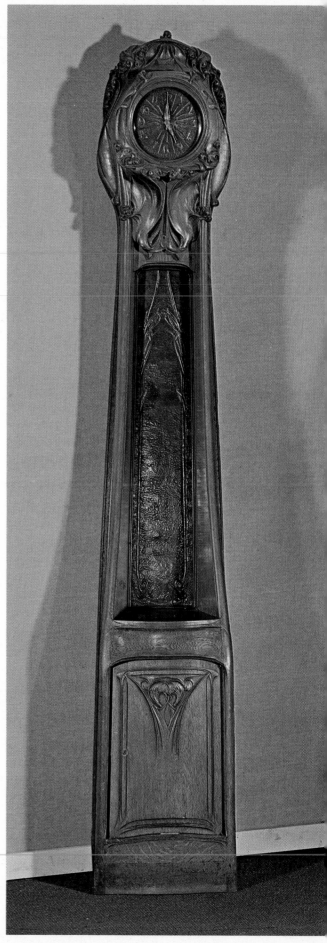

15

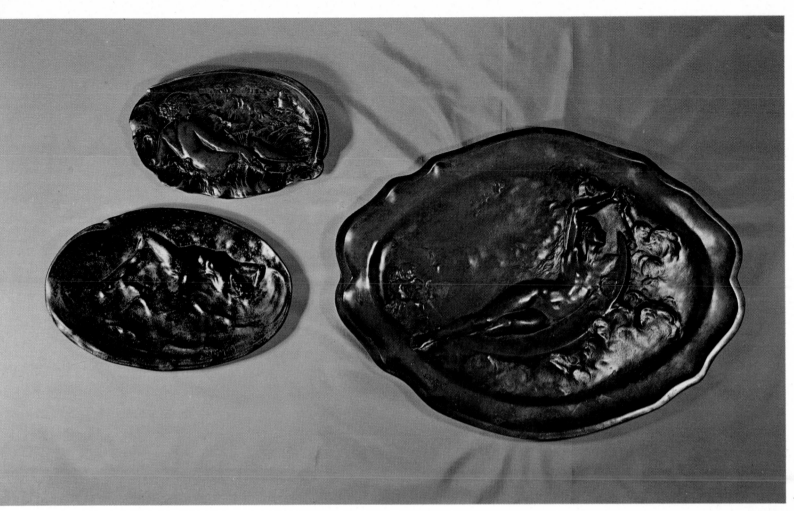

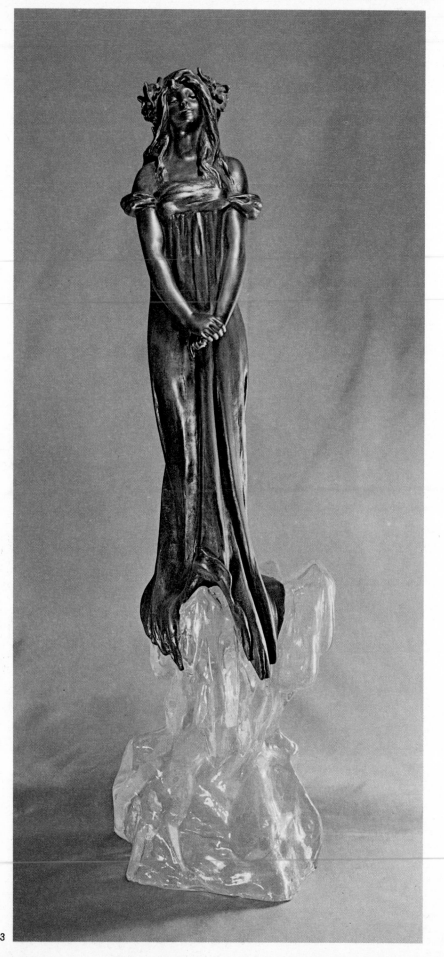

25

26

29

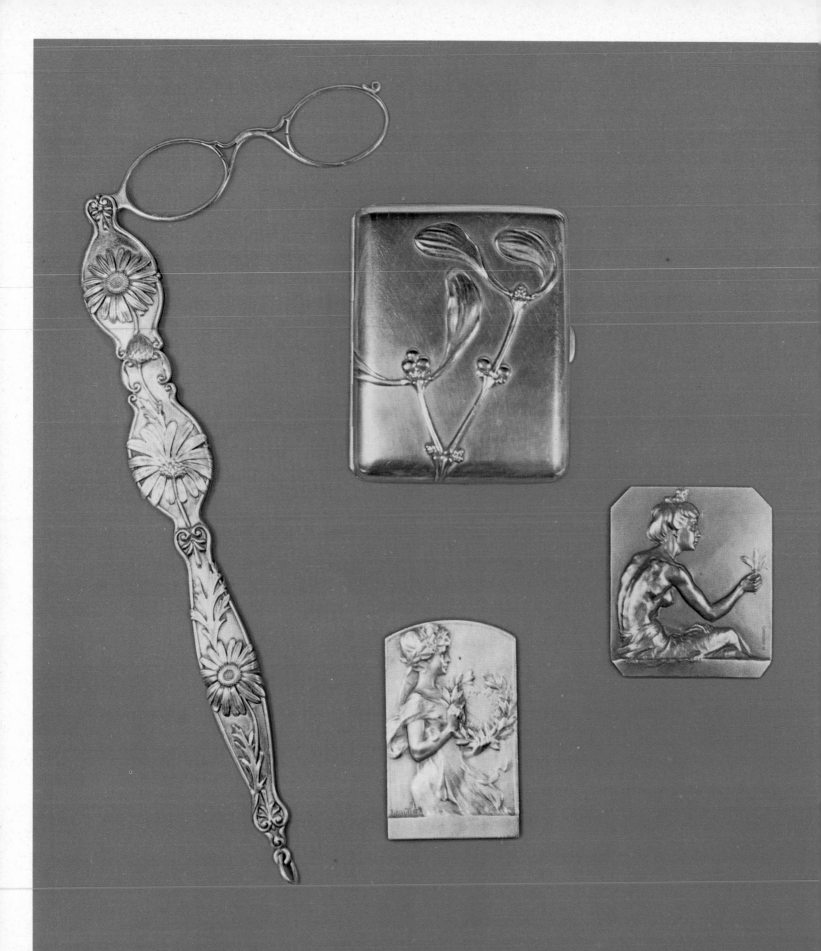

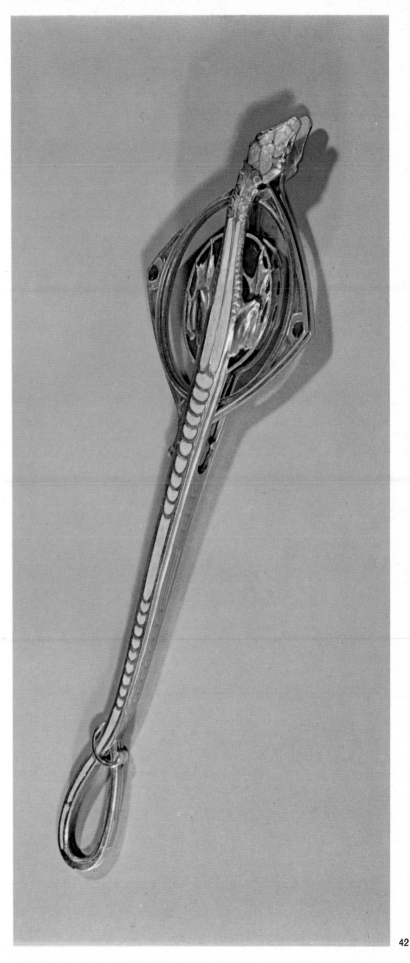

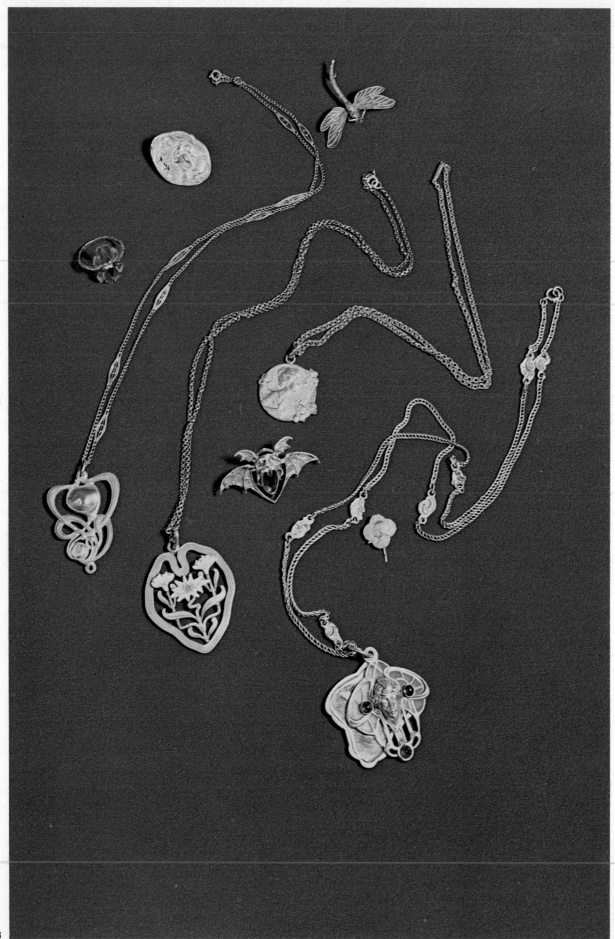

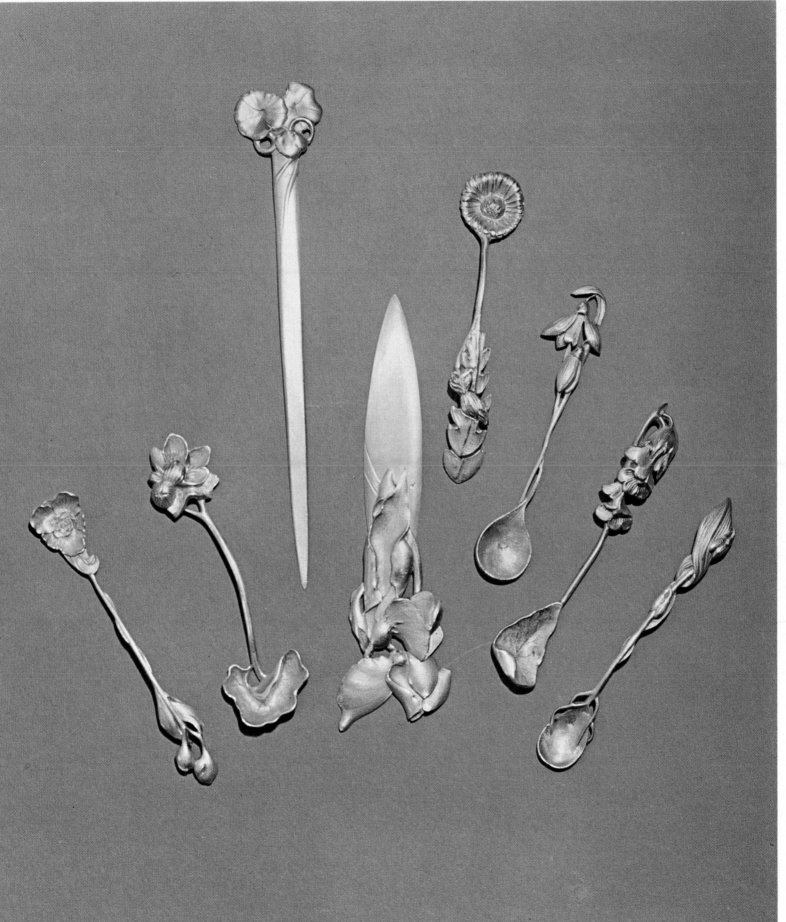

CUERINET 140 Fg St Martin, Paris

Ed. BENEDICTUS. — Iris, tulipes et chrysanthèmes.

49

50

51

52

53